I0477352

# DATING IN THE DIGITAL AGE

## DIGITAL AGE

### MYTHS AND TRUTHS
### OF FINDING LOVE ONLINE

**DAVID SANDUA**

Dating in the digital age. Myths and truths of finding love online.
© David Sandua 2024. All rights reserved.
Electronic and paperback edition.

*"Online dating is not a magic solution;
it's just another tool in the complicated game of love.*

**Mark Manson** *(Author & blogger)*

# INDEX

# I. INTRODUCTION

The rapid evolution of technology has not only reshaped how we communicate but has fundamentally altered our approach to relationships. The advent of online dating platforms has made it more accessible for people to seek companionship, appealing to millions who desire connection in an increasingly fast-paced world. These platforms often tout their ability to match users based on compatibility, with algorithms designed to streamline the search for the perfect partner. The convenience of swiping through potential matches from the comfort of one's home can be alluring, presenting the prospect of love as merely a click away. Despite the allure of instant gratification and tailored connections, this new dating landscape comes with its own set of complexities that merit further examination. While online dating undoubtedly offers opportunities to meet individuals one might not encounter in traditional social settings, it raises significant questions about authenticity and connection. Users often present an idealized version of themselves through curated profiles, leading to a digital façade that can distort perceptions of reality. This phenomenon reveals a critical aspect of online dating: the disparity between genuine human interaction and the superficiality of profile pictures and bios. The reliance on algorithms to influence romantic decisions can foster unrealistic expectations about compatibility and attraction. As individuals navigate this virtual dating scene, understanding the underlying mechanisms of these platforms and their impact on relationship dynamics becomes essential. While the promise of finding love in a few clicks is enticing, the myths surrounding online dating can often overshadow the reality of forming meaningful connections. Many individuals entering the digital dating sphere are unaware of the risks of misrepresentation and the superficial nature of initial interactions. Acknowledging these pitfalls can empower users to engage with these platforms thoughtfully and realistically, fostering healthier relationships. By debunking prevalent misconceptions—such as the notion that a perfect match is simply a profile away—this exploration aims to illuminate the intricacies of online dating. As we navigate this digital era, cultivating a deeper understanding of romantic interactions online will be crucial in redefining love and connection in the modern age.

## Overview of Online Dating Landscape

The allure of online dating platforms primarily stems from their promise of efficiency and convenience in finding companionship. As life becomes increasingly fast-paced, these platforms cater to a generation seeking love amid busy schedules. With just a few clicks, users can access a vast pool of potential partners, each equipped with profiles designed to highlight the most appealing aspects of their personalities and lifestyles. The immediacy of swiping on apps like Tinder or browsing profiles on sites like Match.com creates a sense of excitement; however, this instant gratification can also foster unrealistic expectations. Many users enter the digital dating sphere envisioning quick matches leading to meaningful relationships, unaware that such platforms often prioritize quantity over quality. As a result, while online dating can redefine the way individuals connect, it also raises critical questions about the nature of those connections and the depth of relationships formed through them. Despite its appeal, the online dating landscape is riddled with complexities and challenges that can distort the search for genuine connections. The algorithms employed by these platforms play a pivotal role, often favoring initial physical attraction rather than long-term compatibility. These algorithms analyze user preferences and behaviors, generating match suggestions that may reflect superficial criteria rather than deeper emotional or intellectual compatibility. Consequently, this technological mediation can lead to a culture of disposability, where users quickly swipe past potential matches based on limited criteria, reducing the likelihood of developing meaningful relationships. The reliance on curated profiles and attractive photographs can mask fundamental qualities, fostering a phenomenon known as the paradox of choice. Users overwhelmed by options may find themselves less satisfied with their selections, as they grapple with the idealization of potential partners based solely on their presented personas rather than their true selves. Navigating the online dating sphere also requires an awareness of its inherent risks, particularly concerning authenticity and trust. Many users face the challenge of discerning truth from deception when it comes to the representations individuals make on their profiles. Misleading photographs, fake identities, and exaggerated personal traits can lead to disillusionment, complicating the already challenging quest for love. The superficial nature of interactions can inhibit the development of emotional bonds, reducing relationships to mere entertainment or casual encounters instead of fostering deeper connections. This superficiality is exacerbated by the plethora of choices that online dating presents, often leaving individuals longing for more meaningful dialogue and shared experiences that transcend the screen. In recognizing these complexities, it becomes imperative for users to approach online dating with a balanced perspective, taking care to implement strategies that promote authenticity while remaining aware of the limitations that these platforms present in forming genuine romantic relationships.

## Purpose and Scope of the Essay

In examining the intricacies of online dating platforms, it becomes evident that the myths surrounding these technologies often overshadow their potential. Many users are lured by the promise of a convenient and efficient means of finding a partner, yet they frequently overlook the complexities embedded in these interactions. The essay delves into the distinction between the idealized portrayals of online dating and the actual experiences reported by users. Statistical evidence, along with anecdotal accounts, reviews the unexpected consequences of such platforms, shedding light on the phenomenon of superficial connections that are often formed at the expense of deeper, more meaningful relationships. By unpacking both the seductive allure and the potential pitfalls of online dating, the paper aims to provide a balanced perspective that challenges the prevailing myths and encourages more nuanced engagement with these technologies. The exploration of algorithms reveals how they shape not only the outcomes of matches but also users perceptions of desirability and compatibility. Dating apps rely heavily on data analysis and behavioral patterns to provide personalized suggestions, yet this system can inadvertently narrow individuals choices and foster unrealistic expectations. The expectation that users can find their "perfect match" based on a few metrics does not account for the complexities of human relationships, which cannot merely be quantified or commodified. When analyzed through empirical studies, it becomes apparent that the algorithms used in these platforms prioritize engagement over authenticity, often leading to relationships based on surface-level characteristics rather than genuine emotional connection. This critical examination invites readers to reconsider the efficacy of online matchmaking systems and their influence on the modern pursuit of love. The recommendations synthesizing the findings of this essay are intended to guide individuals in navigating the digital dating landscape more effectively. By acknowledging the limitations of online profiles and being vigilant about the authenticity of the information presented, users can cultivate a more realistic approach to dating in the digital realm. The insights provided suggest adopting a mindful attitude towards interactions, utilizing these platforms not as beacons of certainty in the search for love, but rather as tools that exist within a broader social context. This essay underscores the importance of fostering awareness regarding the myths and realities of online dating, empowering users to engage with these platforms more consciously. Through informed choices and a critical approach, individuals can enhance their experiences and potentially discover more fulfilling relationships in an otherwise overwhelming digital landscape.

## Importance of Understanding Myths and Truths

In the age of online dating, misperceptions proliferate regarding how relationships are formed and sustained. Users often fall prey to the myth that algorithms can perfectly match them with their ideal partners, creating an unrealistic expectation of a seamless romantic experience. Understanding the distinction between this myth and the truth—that algorithms primarily analyze data without the nuance of human emotions—can greatly impact how individuals approach their searches. Research shows that while compatibility scores can provide guidance, the serendipity of real-life interactions and the complexities of human behavior cannot be fully captured by even the most advanced technology. Recognizing this gap can help users shift their perspective, focusing less on finding the one and more on establishing meaningful connections that can evolve over time, thereby fostering healthier relationships rooted in realistic expectations. Exploring the motivations behind online dating reveals another layer of complexity. The appeal of these platforms is not solely about finding love; its also tied to the desire for validation and social engagement. Many users enter the online dating sphere believing they can quickly find romance, yet they often overlook the importance of personal growth and understanding their own needs. The act of dating online can sometimes prioritize superficial judgments based on profile pictures and brief bios, thereby hindering the depth of personal interactions. By examining the truths surrounding these motivations, individuals can reframe their online dating strategies. Rather than pursuing a series of fleeting encounters, users should seek to cultivate self-awareness and communicate openly about their intentions, leading to more meaningful connections. This shift in mindset emphasizes the necessity of patience and the recognition that every interaction can contribute to personal development, regardless of its outcome. Dispelling myths surrounding online dating equips individuals with the tools necessary for a more fulfilling experience. When users acknowledge these distortions, they can better navigate the often overwhelming landscape of digital romance. Many believe that only physical attraction matters; however, substantial research points to emotional compatibility being equally, if not more, important in sustaining long-term relationships. By understanding the interplay between these elements, users can create more robust frameworks for their interactions. This knowledge can transform potentially frustrating search experiences into opportunities for growth and connection. Encouraging a mindset rooted in realistic expectations, open communication, and emotional intelligence not only protects users from disappointment but also promotes healthier dynamics within the overarching context of online dating, ultimately leading to more favorable outcomes in the quest for love in the digital age.

# II. HISTORY OF DATING

The evolution of romantic relationships mirrors the broader shifts in societal norms and technological advancements throughout history. From arranged marriages and societal prescriptions of courtship, the landscape of dating has undergone profound changes. In earlier times, relationships were primarily dictated by social status and family alliances, often leaving personal choice at the periphery. With the rise of individualism in the 18th and 19th centuries, particularly through the Romantic movement, the notion of love evolved into a more personal and intimate pursuit. Dating, as a concept, emerged, allowing individuals to engage in social interactions without the binding constraints of family expectations. This shift is significant as it laid the foundation for the more liberal attitudes toward dating we see today, especially as the 20th century ushered in cultural revolutions that emphasized personal happiness and emotional fulfillment in romantic partnerships. As the 20th century progressed, the landscape of dating continued to transform, reflecting changes in social dynamics, particularly through the impact of mass media. The introduction of dating norms such as going "steady" in the 1950s or the advent of the "dating culture" in the 1960s marked a period of exploration and experimentation in romantic relationships. The influence of television and films began to shape perceptions of courtship, offering idealized visions of love that were often unattainable in reality. Concurrently, the sexual revolution challenged traditional views, encouraging more open and casual dating practices. These cultural shifts also cultivated unrealistic expectations about romance and partnerships, which have persisted into contemporary dating practices. This complex history reflects how popular culture can shape individual desires and expectations, leading to a persistent search for "the perfect match," a theme echoed in modern online dating platforms. In recent decades, technology has reshaped romantic pursuits significantly, with the arrival of dating apps and online platforms revolutionizing the search for companionship. The convenience of swiping through potential matches has created a sense of immediacy and accessibility that appeals to many. Yet, this rapid-fire method of connection often sacrifices depth for speed, with users frequently faced with the dilemma of navigating superficial judgments based solely on profiles and images. Research suggests that while online dating can broaden opportunities for finding love, it may also lead to a diminished sense of true connection as individuals become accustomed to ephemeral encounters. The challenge lies in balancing the excitement of modern technology with the inherent desire for meaningful, lasting relationships. Addressing these complexities has become essential in understanding the realities of dating in the digital age, emphasizing the need for users to approach platforms with both an open heart and a critical mind.

## Evolution of Courtship Practices

Throughout history, the methods and norms surrounding courtship have undergone transformative changes, reflecting broader societal shifts in technology, culture, and gender roles. In pre-industrial societies, courtship was often a communal affair, with families and social networks playing vital roles in matchmaking. This period emphasized practicality over romance, where marriages were frequently arranged to ensure economic stability and social alliance. As societies progressed into the modern era, the rise of individualism shifted romantic pursuits from familial arrangements to personal choice. With the advent of the industrial revolution, young adults began to seek partners through social gatherings, highlighting an evolving emphasis on romantic love as a primary motive for marriage. This evolution marked a significant departure from utilitarian partnerships, paving the way for romantic relationships built on personal affinity and emotional connection. The introduction of new technologies has dramatically influenced courtship practices, particularly from the late 20th century onward. With the rise of the internet and mobile communication, traditional dating norms began to erode, giving way to an era defined by virtual interactions. Online platforms emerged as pivotal spaces for singles to explore romantic possibilities beyond their immediate social circles, offering anonymity and accessibility. This sample democratization of dating significantly altered how individuals present themselves to potential partners. Profiles curated with carefully selected images and key phrases allow users to project idealized versions of themselves, often leading to a disparity between online personas and real-life identities. As such, dating apps have reframed courtship not only as an exploration of personal connections but also as a performance where the stakes are high due to the competitive nature of these platforms. Implications of the digital shift in courtship extend beyond merely the means of connection; they raise critical questions about the nature of romantic relationships in contemporary society. Superficial interactions often dominate initial encounters, where compatibility is frequently assessed through concise characteristics and visual appeal, rather than deeper emotional or intellectual engagement. This immediate gratification can distort the perception of love, reducing it to transactional encounters rather than meaningful partnerships. Users frequently engage in a paradox of choice—overwhelmed by numerous potential matches, they may struggle to commit to one partner, leading to disposable relationships. As the digital age continues to redefine romantic landscapes, it is essential to cultivate a critical awareness of these practices. By approaching online dating with realistic expectations and a focus on genuine connections, individuals can navigate this complex terrain and foster more rewarding and sincere relationships.

## Introduction of Online Dating Platforms

The emergence of online dating platforms has fundamentally transformed the landscape of modern relationships, providing an unprecedented opportunity for individuals to connect across geographical and social barriers. Users are drawn to the convenience of match-making algorithms that curate potential partners based on shared interests, values, and preferences. This new era of romance allows individuals to expand their dating pool beyond traditional social settings, creating interactions that may not have happened otherwise. For many, the allure of finding love or companionship at their fingertips has transformed dating from a daunting venture into an accessible experience. The complexities behind these platforms often lead to misunderstandings regarding their actual efficacy in fostering genuine connections. The reliance on digital interfaces raises important questions about the nature of attraction and the superficiality that may arise within online interactions. Profiles are often enhanced with curated images and carefully crafted descriptions, leading participants to present idealized versions of themselves, a phenomenon known as catfishing. This emphasis on visual appeal can overshadow deeper qualities, such as compatibility and shared values, ultimately skewing perceptions of potential relationships. Consequently, users may find themselves in a paradox where the search for love becomes entangled with unrealistic expectations and filtered realities. While online platforms can facilitate introductions that may develop into meaningful connections, appreciating the nuance of each interaction is crucial to avoid falling victim to a false sense of romantic fulfillment. In navigating the complexities of online dating, an awareness of these dynamics is vital for anyone seeking meaningful relationships. The trajectory from initial interest to a lasting partnership involves more than just clicking through profiles; it requires critical self-reflection and honest communication. Users should approach these platforms with a balanced mindset, understanding the limitations of digital interactions while being open to the possibilities they present. Engaging with potential partners in a mindful manner can lead to healthier connections, allowing individuals to transcend the myths that often surround electronic romance. By cultivating realistic expectations and valuing authenticity, users can enhance their online dating experiences while constructing relationships grounded in reality rather than the transient nature of digital encounters.

## Cultural Shifts in Dating Norms

The evolution of dating norms in recent years has been significantly influenced by the advent of technology and social media platforms, which have fundamentally altered how individuals approach romantic relationships. Traditionally, societal expectations dictated a slower, more structured approach to courtship, often involving familial approval and social rituals. The digital landscape has ushered in an era where instant communication and the ease of connecting with diverse individuals have led to a more informal style of dating. Online dating apps, featuring user-driven profiles and geographical filters, allow people to swipe through potential partners, fostering a culture that prioritizes quick judgments based on visual appeal. This shift has transformed the way individuals prioritize traits that were once deemed essential, such as compatibility and shared values, often leading to a superficial approach to relationship-building, where first impressions dominate over deeper connections. In addition to altering perceptions of potential partners, the digitization of dating has also reshaped societal norms surrounding the frequency and nature of romantic encounters. Unlike previous generations, where dating often implied exclusivity and a commitment to long-term relationships, contemporary dating culture sees individuals engaging in multiple connections simultaneously. This practice, frequently termed situationships, reflects a broader cultural shift toward valuing personal autonomy and immediate gratification over traditional progression toward commitment. The paradox lies in the simultaneous rise of modern datings fluidity and the potential for emotional ramifications, such as increased anxiety and fear of rejection. As people navigate this new landscape shaped by rapidly changing expectations, the challenge becomes balancing the quest for connection with the need for authenticity, leading many to question the sustainability of such transient encounters in the search for lasting love. The implications of these cultural shifts extend beyond individual experiences, influencing broader societal perceptions of love and relationships. The prevalence of online dating platforms has introduced an unprecedented level of choice, enticing users into believing that a perfect partner is always just a swipe away. This concept of limitless possibilities can lead to the phenomenon known as choice overload, where individuals find themselves paralyzed by options and less satisfied with their choices. The curated nature of online profiles presents an idealized version of self that may contradict one's true identity, complicating the quest for meaningful connections. As the myths surrounding online dating are debunked—such as the idea that one should always be looking for the one—it becomes essential to foster realistic expectations and engage in genuine communication. As users navigate this evolving landscape, they must reconcile the tension between the allure of digital romance and the yearning for authentic, deep-rooted relationships.

# III. THE RISE OF ONLINE DATING

With the advent of technology, the cultural landscape of romance has shifted considerably. Traditional dating methods, characterized by face-to-face interactions and organic courtship, have given way to online platforms that enhance accessibility and choice. This transition highlights a fundamental change in how individuals perceive compatibility and attraction. Rather than relying solely on serendipitous encounters or introductions through mutual friends, many now turn to dating apps and websites for a curated selection of potential partners. The gamification of dating, wherein users swipe left or right based on visual cues and brief profiles, has attracted millions. This approach taps into the human desire for instant gratification and immediacy, but it simultaneously poses challenges regarding the depth of connections. While the promise of a perfect match at one's fingertips is alluring, it often oversimplifies the complex nature of building meaningful relationships. Despite its widespread acceptance, the online dating phenomenon is not devoid of consequences. The reliance on algorithms designed to match users based on shared preferences and interests can create a distorted view of intimacy. These algorithms can inadvertently promote superficial judgments, as users often base their interests on limited information gleaned from profiles and photos. This reduction of potential partners to mere data points can lead to disappointing encounters when individuals meet in person. Consequently, many users may find themselves disillusioned, confronting a stark contrast between their online experiences and the reality of in-person interactions. The curated nature of online profiles can mask essential personality traits, fostering a false sense of security that can damage the foundation of mutual trust necessary for any successful relationship. As such, while online dating can broaden one's social horizon, it also underscores the importance of approaching such platforms with awareness and caution. Navigating the complex landscape of online dating requires a nuanced understanding of its implications for interpersonal connections. Those seeking love in the digital realm must remain vigilant about the possibility of misinformation, as profiles can often contain exaggerations or omissions that skew perceptions. Individuals should cultivate realistic expectations about the online dating experience, recognizing that the path to meaningful relationships is rarely linear. To avoid potential pitfalls, users should invest time into getting to know their matches beyond surface-level interactions. Engaging in conversations that explore values, life experiences, and emotional readiness can uncover deeper compatibility that transcends algorithmic matches. Fostering connections in this digital age necessitates a balance of enthusiasm and discernment, encouraging users to embrace the benefits of technology while maintaining a critical eye. Through mindful engagement, individuals can navigate the complexities of online dating more effectively, breaking free from myths that often obscure the potential for genuine love.

## Statistics on Online Dating Usage

In recent years, online dating has seen a remarkable surge in popularity, particularly among younger demographics. Surveys indicate that approximately 30% of U.S. adults have used an online dating platform at some point in their lives, with this figure rising to around 50% for those aged 18 to 29. The proliferation of dating apps has democratized the dating scene, allowing people from diverse backgrounds and locations to connect with potential partners who they may never have met otherwise. Approximately one-third of individuals who have used these platforms report having entered into a committed relationship as a result. This statistic suggests that while skepticism exists regarding the effectiveness of online dating, many users do find meaningful connections, challenging the belief that digital interactions cannot lead to genuine romance. The wide array of choices available on these platforms reflects both the ease and challenges of modern dating, as users navigate a marketplace of personalities through profile pictures and bios. Algorithms play a critical role in shaping the online dating experience, tailoring matches to the users preferences and behaviors. Dating platforms utilize sophisticated data analytics that assess user interactions, preferences, and even psychological traits to suggest compatible profiles. Research by the Pew Research Center reveals that around 66% of users believe that the algorithms improve their dating experience by helping them find more suitable matches. This reliance on technology raises questions about the authenticity of connections formed through such facilitated matches. Users may inadvertently prioritize surface-level traits, such as attractiveness or interests highlighted in a profile, over deeper characteristics that contribute to a lasting relationship. While users may initially gravitate towards algorithmically suggested matches, the superficial coding may risk overlooking the complexities of human attraction and compatibility, which do not easily conform to numerical values or categorizations. Despite the enticing allure of convenience and access to a broad pool of potential partners, online dating is not without its pitfalls. Users frequently face issues of deceptive profiles, where individuals might misrepresent themselves through outdated photographs or embellished bios, fostering a culture of superficiality. Data from a recent study indicates that nearly 50% of online daters have encountered someone who misrepresented themselves on a dating platform. This deception can lead to unrealistic expectations and disillusionment when the online persona does not align with the real person. The emphasis on expediency associated with swiping through profiles may reduce the likelihood of developing meaningful connections, as users often engage in what psychologists term rapid-fire dating. While online dating opens the door to a multitude of possibilities, it also necessitates a critical approach to mitigate pitfalls, ensuring that users remain aware of the realities behind the facade.

## Demographics of Online Daters

One crucial aspect of the online dating landscape is its diverse demographic composition. Users range widely in age, gender, ethnicity, and sexual orientation, reflecting the complexities of modern dating. Recent studies indicate that younger generations, particularly those aged 18 to 29, are the most active users of online dating platforms, often driven by a desire for casual relationships or hookups. Older individuals, particularly those in their 30s and 40s, are increasingly adopting these platforms, typically seeking more serious connections. Gender dynamics also play a vital role, with women often approaching online dating from a more cautious perspective, reflecting safety concerns and the potential for objectification. The increasing acceptance of LGBTQ+ relationships has broadened the scope of online dating, as dedicated platforms cater specifically to these communities. This diversity underscores the notion that online dating is not a monolithic experience but rather a multifaceted social phenomenon influenced by various demographic factors. Another significant dimension in understanding online daters involves the socio-economic factors that influence their experiences and choices. Users often come from varying educational backgrounds, income levels, and geographical locations, greatly impacting how they interact with dating platforms. Higher education levels are frequently correlated with the tendency to engage in more meaningful connections, as these individuals may prioritize compatibility over casual encounters. Conversely, users from lower socio-economic backgrounds might gravitate toward those platforms that promise quick connections, possibly due to time constraints related to work and financial stability. Urban residents often have more access to a greater variety of dating apps compared to those living in rural areas, which can limit their options and experiences. This disparity exemplifies how socio-economic factors can dictate not only the choice of platforms but also the overall success and satisfaction in forming relationships through digital means. Cultural influences also play a pivotal role in shaping the demographics of online daters. Individuals attitudes towards dating, relationships, and even technology vary significantly across different cultural backgrounds. In some cultures, traditional courtship practices still prevail, making online dating a relatively new and sometimes controversial concept. Conversely, cultures that emphasize individualism and personal choice might see more widespread acceptance of online platforms as a legitimate means of finding companionship. This divide is not only evident along ethnic lines but also manifests in varying acceptance levels of different relationship types, such as casual dating versus long-term commitments. Consequently, the online dating experience is filtered through a cultural lens, which affects how users present themselves and what they seek from potential partners. This cultural context enriches the discussion surrounding online dating, highlighting that it is not merely a technological advancement but also a reflection of ongoing changes in societal norms and values.

## Popular Platforms and Their Features

Among the extensive range of dating platforms available today, some have emerged as particularly popular due to their distinct features that cater to various user needs. Tinder, often recognized for its swiping mechanism, prioritizes user experience by providing an engaging interface that emphasizes immediacy and visual appeal. This app has capitalized on the notion of "love at first sight," allowing users to make quick judgments based primarily on photos, which can often lead to superficial connections. By contrast, platforms like eHarmony focus on compatibility through a more in-depth profile creation process that engages users in completing extensive questionnaires aimed at matching them based on personality traits and values. This variance highlights the necessity for users to align their expectations with the features of the platform they choose, as each caters to different approaches of interaction, from the casual to the serious. User safety is another significant feature that varies among dating apps, often influencing the decision-making process for potential matches. Leading platforms such as Bumble have taken proactive measures to establish a more secure dating environment by allowing women to initiate conversations, thereby reducing instances of unwanted messages and harassment. By prioritizing the empowerment of users, Bumble not only cultivates healthier interactions but also enhances overall trust in online dating experiences. Meanwhile, others like OkCupid offer transparency by presenting percentage-match scores based on users' answers to relationship-oriented questions. This feature fosters a sense of accountability among users, empowering them to make informed decisions. The discrepancy in safety measures across platforms underscores an essential consideration for users: the importance of selecting a platform that aligns with their preferences regarding safety features and community engagement. The diverse characteristics of popular dating platforms reflect the multifaceted nature of online dating itself, raising questions about the efficacy of these features in fostering genuine connections. While platforms provide tools that can significantly enhance the dating experience by facilitating new social interactions, the superficiality often encouraged by some apps can lead to disillusionment among users seeking meaningful relationships. The reliance on algorithms to generate matches can obscure the complexity of human relationships, reducing them to mere numbers and statistics. As it stands, the choice of platform should be carefully considered, with users remaining cognizant of how features influence their experiences and expectations. In navigating the digital dating landscape, the balance between utilizing the benefits offered by these platforms and recognizing their limitations ultimately shapes one's success in finding authentic love in the online realm.

# IV. MYTH: ONLINE DATING IS ONLY FOR DESPERATE PEOPLE

The notion that online dating is primarily for those who are desperate is a misconception rooted in stigma and outdated perceptions of romantic pursuits. In reality, individuals from diverse backgrounds and varying relationship experiences are increasingly turning to digital platforms to seek companionship. A survey conducted by the Pew Research Center reveals that nearly 30% of U.S. adults have used online dating tools, and a significant portion of these users report finding meaningful relationships. The reasons for venturing into this realm are often practical: busy schedules, geographic limitations, and a desire to meet individuals outside one's immediate social circle can all contribute to the choice of online dating. Instead of desperation, many users view these platforms as efficient, contemporary tools that align with their lifestyles, showcasing a shift in how society perceives romantic engagement. Another aspect that challenges the myth of desperation is the increasing normalization of online dating in popular culture. Once considered taboo, online dating has permeated various media, depicting successful, happy relationships emerging from digital introductions. This cultural shift is influential; it encourages individuals to embrace technology as a viable avenue for forming romantic connections. Studies indicate that online dating can foster more successful matches than traditional methods, as algorithms are designed to pair users based on shared interests and values rather than mere physical attraction. Access to data-driven insights allows for more thoughtful engagement, encouraging users to evaluate compatibility more critically. As such, the stigma around online dating has been significantly reduced, with more individuals viewing it as a legitimate and effective means of finding love rather than a last resort. In addition to culture and practicality, psychological factors play a significant role in dispelling the myth that online dating is exclusively for the desperate. Many individuals who utilize digital platforms possess a proactive stance toward their romantic lives, opting to explore various avenues to meet potential partners. This approach aligns with modern attitudes towards agency and choice in relationships—users often prefer to take control of their dating experiences rather than solely relying on fate or chance encounters. The ability to engage in online communication before meeting in person can ease social anxieties and help users build confidence in navigating romantic relationships. This proactive mentality underscores the notion that online dating is not a desperate act but rather a strategic choice in the quest for companionship. Through these different lenses, it becomes evident that online dating is not about desperation but about embracing opportunities for connection in an increasingly digital world.

## Misconceptions About Online Daters

The landscape of online dating is often clouded with preconceived notions that can skew perceptions of the experience. One prevalent belief is that users of online dating platforms are solely looking for casual relationships or hookups. This stereotype overlooks the diverse motivations that individuals bring to these platforms. Research indicates that a significant number of users are genuinely interested in long-term companionship and meaningful connections. Factors such as busy lifestyles, geographic mobility, and varied personal circumstances can drive people to explore these digital options, often realizing that traditional dating avenues may not be feasible or effective. By framing online daters as merely seeking superficial encounters, society both alienates those looking for deeper bonds and diminishes the legitimacy of their pursuit of love in this modern context. There is a misconception that online dating is primarily a young persons arena, which neglects the positive experiences of older adults in this space. Many assume that younger generations possess the digital savvy necessary for successful online dating, while older individuals remain technologically inept and resistant to change. Conversely, studies reveal that a growing number of older adults are embracing these platforms, finding solace in the ability to connect with like-minded individuals post-divorce or following the loss of a partner. They often value the convenience, safety, and broader options that online dating provides. As these mature users become increasingly prevalent, the narrative surrounding age and online dating needs to evolve. This shift can help dismantle the stigma faced by older users, fostering a more inclusive environment for individuals of all ages seeking companionship and love. The notion that profiles and photographs accurately represent a persons true self is deeply misleading. Many individuals curate their online presence, consciously highlighting certain attributes while downplaying or omitting others. This has led to a proliferation of filtered images and idealized portrayals that can distort the reality of who someone truly is. The psychological phenomenon known as the "halo effect" can further complicate this dynamic, where attractive individuals are often presumed to possess positive personality traits. Consequently, users may find themselves navigating a landscape laden with representations that prioritize aesthetics over authenticity. In recognizing this aspect of online dating, individuals can approach their interactions with a more discerning attitude, seeking to understand the complex nuances behind curated profiles. Emphasizing the importance of genuine communication can help foster healthier connections and mitigate misunderstandings stemming from superficial impressions.

## Motivations Behind Online Dating

As individuals increasingly turn to online platforms for romantic relationships, a multifaceted array of motivations emerges behind this trend. Many users are driven by convenience, as online dating allows for connection beyond geographic boundaries and traditional social structures. Unlike the past, where individuals might meet potential partners through mutual acquaintances or local events, todays digital landscape offers numerous platforms catering to diverse interests and demographics. This accessibility can be particularly appealing to busy professionals with limited time for in-person socializing, as it allows them to explore potential matches at their own pace. The rise of mobile applications facilitates spontaneous interactions, which can enhance the dating experience and foster connections in real time, thereby broadening the scope of potential relationships. Another significant motivation stems from the search for compatibility, which is often perceived as more manageable through algorithm-driven matchmaking. These algorithms, fueled by user preferences and behavioral patterns, promise to introduce individuals to compatible matches based on shared interests, values, or lifestyle choices. While many users find solace in the notion that technology can guide their search for lasting love, this reliance on algorithms also raises questions about the nature of connection in contemporary relationships. The promise of finding the perfect match can distort expectations, leading users to approach dating with a checklist mentality instead of fostering genuine connections. Consequently, this pursuit for compatibility can unintentionally elevate superficial qualities over emotional intimacy, impacting the quality and depth of relationships formed through dating platforms. The allure of anonymity and the potential for self-expression play a pivotal role in motivating users to engage with online dating. For many, digital platforms offer a space where individuals can curate their identities and present themselves in an appealing manner without the immediate pressures of face-to-face interaction. This aspect can be liberating for those who are shy or who had limited dating experiences in traditional settings. The simultaneous potential for deception complicates this narrative. Users may present idealized versions of themselves, leading to the phenomenon known as catfishing, where individuals create false personas in order to attract others. This dynamic introduces significant risks regarding trust and authenticity in online interactions, necessitating a cautious approach to vulnerable self-presentation. As individuals navigate the digital dating landscape, understanding these motivations is crucial in fostering a more genuine approach to forming emotional connections.

## Success Stories of Online Relationships

In the landscape of online dating, many individuals have discovered lasting partnerships that transcend the original intent of casual interactions. An illustrative case is that of Emily and Jake, who initially connected on a popular dating app. Their journey began solely as a fling during college, with casual banter and occasional meetups. As they continued to communicate, they found shared interests that deepened their relationship beyond the superficiality often associated with online encounters. Over time, their bond solidified through countless late-night conversations, wherein they unveiled vulnerabilities, hopes, and dreams, ultimately leading to a committed relationship that has flourished for over three years. Their success story exemplifies how digital interfaces can serve as gateways to genuine emotional connections, challenging the misconception that online interactions inherently lack depth. Equally compelling are cases involving individuals who have navigated the complexities of online dating to find their lifelong partners. Consider the story of Mia and Liam, who met through a niche dating platform catering to avid travelers. Their mutual passion for exploration facilitated a connection that quickly grew into something profound. After several virtual conversations filled with stories of past adventures, they arranged to meet in Spain, where their initial shared interest in travel blossomed into a love that felt both exciting and supportive. They now maintain a blog chronicling their global adventures together, continually reinforcing their bond through shared experiences. Mia and Liam's relationship challenges the notion that online connections are fleeting, as their success demonstrates the power of aligning core values and interests through online interactions. The experiences of couples like Sarah and Tom illustrate the potential of online dating to bridge significant geographical gaps. They met while participating in a gaming forum; Sarah was in New York, while Tom resided in California. Their friendship, which began with shared gaming sessions, evolved into an enduring relationship over time as they embraced video calls and online date nights to maintain their connection. Despite the distance, they adapted to their unique situation, demonstrating that commitment and creativity can thrive in online relationships. Eventually, they closed the gap by relocating to a shared city, proving that successful online interactions can culminate in real-life partnerships. Their story reinforces the argument that with patience and intentional efforts, individuals can find meaningful love through digital platforms, countering stereotypes that diminish the validity of online relationships.

# V. TRUTH: ONLINE DATING EXPANDS SOCIAL CIRCLES

The advent of online dating has fundamentally shifted the landscape of social interactions, allowing individuals to form connections that would not have been possible in the traditional dating scene. Unlike conventional methods that often confine potential partners to those within immediate social circles, digital platforms enable users to explore vast networks of individuals beyond their familiar environments. This expanded reach has led to the discovery of romantic interests among individuals from diverse backgrounds, cultures, and geographical locations. Research shows that people often find matches who share similar interests or values, even if they may not have crossed paths in their day-to-day lives. As a result, relationships can blossom in unconventional ways, supported by shared affinities rather than geographical proximity, enriching the dating experiences of countless individuals. The algorithms employed by dating platforms play a significant role in facilitating connections that might otherwise remain unacknowledged. Many of these services utilize complex matching systems designed to analyze users' preferences and suggest compatible partners, thereby optimizing the dating experience. While some critiques argue that algorithms limit genuine engagement by fostering superficial connections, it can be argued that they also enhance compatibility by streamlining options and filtering out unlikely matches. As users interact with the platform, they often cultivate a better understanding of their own preferences, which can result in deeper relationships. This continuous feedback loop not only expands social circles but also fosters a greater sense of agency in choosing partners based on compatibility rather than chance encounters in physical spaces. Thus, while the algorithms might introduce a layer of artificiality, they also serve to enrich the dating landscape by making potential connections visible and accessible. The expansion of social circles through online dating does come with its own set of challenges. As individuals engage with multiple profiles and experiences, they may inadvertently fall prey to a hyperlinked approach to relationships, character-ized by a tendency to treat partners as items on a checklist ra-ther than individuals with unique qualities. This phenomenon can lead to a sense of superficiality in interactions, where users prioritize transient encounters over meaningful connections. The reliance on curated profiles may contribute to the distortion of personal authenticity, as individuals feel compelled to present idealized versions of themselves. The consequence is a para-doxical experience where users can feel more isolated despite an increase in potential partners. Thus, while online dating ex-pands social circles in unprecedented ways, it is essential for participants to navigate these platforms with a mindful ap-proach, recognizing the importance of fostering depth amidst an abundance of choice.

## Access to Diverse Dating Pools

The expansion of online dating platforms has created unprece-dented opportunities for individuals to connect with potential partners beyond their immediate social circles. In the past, find-ing a romantic match often relied heavily on geographical and social limitations, leaving many to settle for local options. With the advent of dating apps and websites, these constraints have been significantly diminished, enabling users to interact with a diverse array of individuals from various backgrounds, cultures, and interests. This democratization of dating encourages greater inclusivity while also fostering an environment where users can explore relationships they might not have previously considered. As a result, people are exposed to different perspectives and lifestyles, enriching their dating experiences and broadening their understanding of love and companionship. This enhanced access to diverse dating pools stands as a testament to how technology can reshape personal relationships, promoting a more interconnected and culturally aware approach to dating. While the promise of connecting with a variety of individuals is enticing, it is also crucial to recognize the complexities that come with such diversity. While a wider dating pool can increase the chances of finding a compatible partner, it may also lead to decision fatigue, where the overwhelming quantity of options paradoxically makes individuals less satisfied with their choices. The psychological phenomenon, referred to as the paradox of choice, suggests that an abundance of options can cause anxiety and indecision, ultimately detracting from the dating experience. As users navigate through countless profiles, there is a risk of superficiality taking precedence over deeper connections. This tendency can manifest in rapid swipe-based interactions, where individuals may overlook meaningful qualities in potential partners in favor of quick judgments based on appearances. Consequently, while diversity in dating pools offers exciting possibilities, it also necessitates a mindful approach to ensure that the search for love remains genuine and fulfilling. The implications of tapping into diverse dating pools reverberate beyond individual experiences, influencing broader societal norms surrounding relationships. As users engage with partners from varied backgrounds, they inadvertently challenge and reshape traditional perceptions of compatibility and courtship. This interaction promotes a culture that values openness and adaptability in relationships, potentially leading to more inclusive standards of love. The critical question arises: are these connections grounded in authenticity, or are they merely products of fleeting online interactions? As individuals explore varied dating options, they must remain vigilant about maintaining a sense of self-awareness and emotional intelligence. Understanding ones values and relationship goals can help navigate the diverse landscape of online dating while mitigating the risks associated with superficial encounters. By emphasizing genuine connections over mere expansion of options, users can better harness the potential of diverse dating pools and cultivate meaningful relationships in the digital age.

## Opportunities for Meeting Like-Minded Individuals

In the landscape of online dating, one of the most significant advantages is the ability to connect with like-minded individuals across vast geographic distances. Traditional dating methods often limited ones options to local social circles, where shared interests might not necessarily align. Platforms designed specifically for dating enable users to filter potential partners based on specific criteria—ranging from lifestyle preferences to values and hobbies. This filtering process is particularly instrumental for individuals seeking relationships that align with their personal beliefs or passions, such as environmentalism, fitness, or specific cultural interests. By engaging with others who share similar priorities, users can foster deeper connections right from the start. Many of these platforms also include discussion forums and interest-specific groups, providing even greater opportunities for individuals to expand their social network and potentially discover romantic connections that might otherwise remain undiscovered in a local context. Unlike traditional avenues, which can often feel contrived or limited, online platforms offer a casual environment conducive to authentic interaction. This accessibility can lead to organic conversations and meaningful exchanges, thereby allowing users to express their true selves without the constraints of in-person social expectations. Virtual spaces encourage a level of openness that is less achievable in conventional settings. Participants can take their time crafting messages that reveal their personalities, which can lead to a more accurate representation of oneself. This sense of freedom can be especially beneficial for introverted individuals or those who find socializing in person daunting. Consequently, the online milieu not only enhances chances of meeting compatible partners but also prepares them to engage meaningfully when transitioning to real-life interactions. Such environments facilitate genuine interest and exploration, ultimately driving more significant relationship outcomes. While the potential for meeting like-minded individuals is vast, it is vital to remain cautious and mindful of the inherent risks associated with online dating. Profiles can be deceiving, often emphasizing idealized versions of oneself that may not align with reality. Some users may approach encounters with a superficial mindset, seeking immediate gratification rather than a meaningful connection. Hence, it becomes crucial for individuals to practice discernment when navigating the world of online relationships. Using the filter features thoughtfully—focusing on more than just physical

attributes—can guide users toward deeper interactions. Understanding the nuances of digital communication can mitigate
misconceptions and enhance the likelihood of forming genuine
bonds. While online dating platforms present unparalleled opportunities to connect with like-minded individuals, a balanced
and reflective approach is essential to harness their full potential and cultivate authentic, fulfilling relationships.

# Geographic Flexibility in Dating

In the contemporary dating landscape, individuals often find
themselves navigating the intricacies of geographic flexibility, a
significant aspect that reshapes romantic possibilities. With the
advent of dating apps and online platforms, people are no
longer limited to potential partners within their immediate vicinity. This geographic flexibility not only broadens their dating
pool but also introduces a diverse array of cultures, values, and
lifestyles, allowing for relationships that might not otherwise
have materialized. As users swipe through profiles, they gain
access to connections that span cities, states, and even coun-
tries, pushing the traditional boundaries that once defined lo-
cale-based dating. While this opens up exciting prospects, it
also raises questions regarding logistics, emotional investment,
and the viability of long-distance relationships. The implications
of geographic flexibility in dating extend beyond mere accessibility; they also influence the expectations that individuals bring
to relationships. The promise of finding love from a broader demographic often creates a pressure to prioritize novelty over
deeper connections. Users may experience a sense of paradox;
the very tools designed to foster meaningful relationships can
lead to superficial engagements propelled by a constant search

for the next best match. As profiles are curated and interactions reduced to digital exchanges, the authenticity of potential connections can become obscured. Its essential to recognize that while geographic flexibility may present numerous options, it does not guarantee emotional compatibility or shared values, which are critical components of successful relationships. The vastness of the dating landscape may contribute to an overwhelming feeling of abundance, leading to commitment issues or a dismissal of genuinely suitable partners. The consequences of geographic flexibility manifest not only in the mechanics of dating but also in the psychological aspects of online interactions. Many individuals embark on journeys with the hope of discovering profound connections, only to confront the challenges inherent to long-distance dynamics, such as communication barriers and differing life schedules. These hurdles can strain relationships, leading to misunderstandings and unmet expectations. Consequently, the allure of geographic flexibility may unintentionally cultivate a culture of impatience; motivated by the ease of access to potential matches, individuals may fail to invest the necessary time and effort into cultivating deeper relationships. By acknowledging these complexities, users can adopt a more reflective approach to their online dating experiences. Striking a balance between enjoying the freedom to explore distant connections while remaining grounded in the reality of relationship-building is pivotal for fostering authentic and enduring partnerships in the digital age.

# VI. MYTH: ALL PROFILES ARE DECEPTIVE

In the realm of online dating, the perception that all profiles are inherently deceptive is a sweeping generalization that overlooks the authenticity that many users strive to present. Although it is not uncommon for individuals to embellish certain aspects of their profiles, the assumption that deception is the norm fails to recognize the diverse motivations behind profile creation. Many users present genuine reflections of their identities, aiming to attract compatible partners with whom they can forge a meaningful connection. Research indicates that authenticity in profiles can lead to more successful matches, as individuals increasingly prioritize honesty and transparency over superficiality. Thus, while some users may indeed misrepresent themselves, it is reductive to label the entirety of online profiles as deceptive. The search for love online encompasses a broad spectrum of intentions and behaviors, and many participants genuinely seek sincere connections. The rise of online dating platforms has not only provided a space for authenticity but has also spurred a culture of mutual accountability among users. The rapid evolution of these platforms has encouraged individuals to engage more meaningfully and to verify the identities of potential matches. Many dating apps now include features such as video chats or photo verification to enhance trust and reduce the likelihood of deception. These practices create an environment where users feel empowered to present their true selves while also assessing the authenticity of others. In this context, accountability and transparency become integral components of the online dating experience. Consequently, rather than viewing profiles as inherently deceptive, users can appreciate the shifts toward more reliable interactions. The nuance in this landscape reveals that many individuals enter the online dating arena with the genuine intent of finding lasting connections. The narrative surrounding online profiles is greatly influenced by societal perceptions of attractiveness and the pressure to conform to idealized images. The need for users to stand out in a crowded digital marketplace can lead some to exaggerate or misrepresent aspects of their lives. This does not imply that all profiles are devoid of truth; many individuals navigate this complexity with integrity, seeking to present themselves authentically amid the pressures of a visually driven medium. Studies indicate that users are often more inclined to engage with profiles that exhibit relatable vulnerabilities instead of unattainable perfection. This shift in perspective underscores the importance of fostering a dating culture that values honesty and self-acceptance, ultimately leading to more fulfilling relationships. By addressing the myth that all profiles are deceptive, we can shift the focus toward fostering genuine connections, urging individuals to embrace authenticity in their online dating experiences.

## Understanding Profile Authenticity

In the context of online dating, the notion of authenticity is increasingly paramount. Users navigate a complex landscape where profiles may not accurately represent the individuals behind them. Many daters curate their online images, leading to discrepancies between how they present themselves and their real-life identities. Research has shown that individuals often gravitate towards photos that highlight their most flattering features, resulting in an idealized version of themselves. This phenomenon underscores the inherent tension between self-presentation and genuine connection; potential partners may find themselves ensnared in a cycle of superficial assessments based solely on visual cues. Authenticity in this digital realm, therefore, becomes a multi-layered challenge, as users must learn to negotiate between the curated personas they see and the authentic interactions they desire. The implications of this disconnect extend beyond mere misunderstandings between users. When individuals encounter profiles that may be deceptive or exaggerated, they may experience heightened levels of skepticism and disappointment in the dating process. Trust is a critical cornerstone of any relationship, and when these profiles fail to resonate with reality, it undermines the foundation that such connections are built upon. Studies have indicated that behaviors such as catfishing, or creating a false persona to deceive others, can lead to serious emotional ramifications for both the deceiver and the deceived. Profiles that lack integrity not only jeopardize the prospect of a meaningful relationship but also perpetuate a cycle where users become increasingly guarded and cynical. By fostering an environment where authenticity is prioritized, dating platforms can pave the way for deeper, more rewarding romantic connections. To navigate the complexities of online dating, it is essential for individuals to adopt a critical lens when evaluating profiles. Awareness of the inherent limitations of digital representations can empower users to approach dating with realistic expectations. Engaging in broader conversations about authenticity can aid in cultivating a more discerning mindset, encouraging daters to prioritize communication and connection over curated visuals. This shift in perspective promotes the understanding that true compatibility extends far beyond surface-level attributes. Users should be encouraged to invest time in getting to know potential partners more mean-ingfully, utilizing initial online interactions as an entry point ra-ther than a definitive judgment of character. Thus, as individuals learn to decode the subtleties of profile authenticity, they will likely foster connections that align more closely with their gen-uine emotional needs and desires, enhancing their overall expe-rience in the digital dating landscape.

## The Role of Self-Presentation

In the context of dating, self-presentation plays a pivotal role in shaping the initial perceptions someone forms about another person. Users of online dating platforms often curate their pro-files meticulously, selecting images and crafting bios that reflect an idealized version of themselves. This means strategically showcasing attributes that might attract potential partners, of-ten emphasizing physical appearance or specific interests. The way individuals choose to present themselves online creates a performative dimension to dating, which can lead to significant disparities between who they are offline and the persona they project digitally. This dissonance raises questions about authen-ticity in relationships, challenging the notion that connections based solely on curated representations can lead to meaningful engagement. Consequently, users must grapple with the dual challenge of presenting themselves attractively while remaining true to their identities—an endeavor that can complicate the foundational trust necessary for building lasting connections. The implications of self-presentation extend beyond personal profiles, influencing the dynamics of communication between users. Research indicates that the way individuals articulate their thoughts, express humor, or even engage in banter can affect their perceived desirability. Users often feel pressure to maintain the facade established during the initial self-presentation stages, leading to a continuous cycle of validation-seeking behavior. This can result in a paradox where the initial excitement of matched interests and mutual attraction morphs into anxiety over maintaining that appealing image. As the relationship develops, individuals may feel compelled to uphold the curated aspects of their personality to match their partner's expectations. This dynamic can inhibit genuine connection, causing individuals to hold back their true selves out of fear that their unfiltered nature will not live up to the polished versions presented online. The role of self-presentation in online dating raises critical concerns about the nature of romantic relationships in the digital age. While participants may initially gravitate towards profiles that align with their ideals, the ensuing interactions are often predicated on an illusion that may falter once faced with reality. This creates a cycle where superficial judgments based on images and carefully crafted messages overshadow deeper compatibility and shared values. As users engage in a transactional approach to dating, they risk reducing relationships to mere evaluations of desirability rather than authentic connections grounded in mutual respect and understanding. To cultivate more meaningful relationships in this landscape, individuals must confront the pressures of self-presentation and adopt a more transparent approach to their online interactions, prioritizing authenticity over perfection. By doing so, they can navigate the complexities of digital romance with a greater likelihood of fostering genuine connections that endure beyond the initial encounter.

# Research on Profile Accuracy

The integrity of online dating profiles significantly influences users perceptions and experiences. Research indicates that many individuals present an idealized version of themselves, skewing the reality of their lives and personalities. Photos are often filtered and selected for their best angles, while profile descriptions can exaggerate interests and achievements. This phenomenon, known as self-enhancement, leads to an unrealistic foundation upon which relationships are formed. Studies show that when users engage in this type of self-presentation, the dissonance between expectation and reality can culminate in disappointment when face-to-face interactions occur. The disconnect between an online persona and the individual's true self raises questions about authenticity in digital romance, as users may struggle to reconcile who they are versus who they portray. Such misalignment can result in mistrust and disillusionment, underscoring the need for authenticity in online dating. In exploring profile accuracy, it is essential to understand the implications of these discrepancies on user interactions and overall satisfaction with dating platforms. Research suggests that while initial attraction may be driven by visually appealing images and compelling narratives, lasting connections arise from genuine compatibility and mutual understanding. When the accuracy of profiles is sacrificed for aesthetic or superficial appeal, users may find themselves in fleeting encounters that do not translate into meaningful relationships. This underscores a critical paradox within the online dating culture: users are drawn in by the allure of their counterparts, yet often find that relationships falter once the facade is lifted. Consequently, the promise of finding the one through swift swipes and clicks may lead to experiences that deviate significantly from expectations, prompting a need for users to reflect critically on their motivations and the authenticity they seek in potential partners. To mitigate the drawbacks of inaccurate profiles, several strategies can be employed by users and platform designers alike. First, fostering a culture of honesty by encouraging individuals to present their true selves may enhance user satisfaction and relationship success rates. Platforms can implement features that emphasize authenticity, such as verification processes or prompts to share genuine interests and experiences. Education on the importance of profile accuracy can empower users to approach online dating with realistic expectations. Emphasizing long-term compatibility over initial visual attraction could help shift focus towards meaningful connections. By grounding the process in authenticity and self-awareness, users can navigate their online dating journeys with a more discerning eye, facilitating more genuine interactions and reducing the potential for disappointment precipitated by the gap between expectation and reality.

# VII. TRUTH: PHOTOS CAN BE MISLEADING

In the realm of online dating, the superficial immediacy of photographs often overshadows the deeper qualities that define genuine connection. Many users present themselves through carefully curated images designed to project specific identities or idealized versions of themselves. Social media platforms accentuate this trend, as users often select and edit visuals that align with societal beauty standards, leaving potential partners with distorted perceptions. This phenomenon is not trivial; rather, it sets a misleading tone for initial interactions. Users may enter conversations with preconceived notions based solely on visual impressions, neglecting other critical aspects of compatibility that could foster meaningful relationships. Consequently, the allure of discovering a perfect match becomes less about authentic connection and more about conforming to an artificial standard, calling into question the integrity of online romantic pursuits. The discrepancy between an individuals online representation and their true persona can significantly influence dating outcomes. Studies indicate that a significant number of individuals have exaggerated their attributes in profiles, leading to unfortunate encounters where expectations do not align with reality. When users meet in person, the mismatch between the projected image and actual characteristics can result in disappointment or disillusionment. Such incongruities can exacerbate feelings of mistrust, making it difficult for users to approach future Dating encounters with an open mind. As relationships evolve, the emphasis on physical appearance can diminish the opportunity for deeper emotional connections, overshadowing

53

the qualities that genuinely matter in sustaining a partnership. Thus, recognizing that photos can often mislead is essential for fostering more authentic interactions in this digital dating landscape. Confronting the challenge of misleading visuals in online dating requires a more nuanced understanding and approach to the platforms. Instead of relying solely on profile images for decision-making, users should invest time in uncovering the personality behind the pictures. Engaging in meaningful conversations and asking thoughtful questions can help illuminate whether or not a potential partners online persona aligns with their true character. Taking time to assess dating preferences critically and being open to various forms of attraction can diminish the impact of misleading photographs. Educating oneself about the intricacies of online dating design can also empower users to interact with the platforms more consciously. By promoting a broader perspective on love and connection, individuals can navigate the often superficial nature of digital dating more effectively, ensuring that their pursuit of romance remains grounded in authenticity rather than illusion.

## The Impact of Image Selection

In the context of online dating, the selection of images plays a pivotal role in shaping perceptions and influencing initial attraction. Users often curate their profiles with images that they believe will cast them in the best light, using flattering angles, careful background choices, and sometimes even photo editing. Research indicates that profiles with high-quality images receive significantly more attention, indicating that visual appeal is a key factor in the early stages of attraction. This prioritization of aesthetics can skew perceptions of compatibility, leading individuals to form snap judgments based solely on images rather than considering deeper personality traits or shared interests. As a result, individuals may find themselves engaged in superficial interactions that ultimately do not foster genuine connections. While images undoubtedly capture initial interest, the implications of image selection extend far beyond the first click. The pressure to present an idealized version of oneself can set unrealistic expectations for both parties involved. When users project an exaggerated or misleading version of their personalities through carefully selected images, it can lead to significant disillusionment during in-person meetings. Many individuals report feelings of inadequacy or dissatisfaction when the reality does not match the curated digital persona. This disconnect not only fuels skepticism about online dating platforms but may also contribute to broader societal trends of dissatisfaction in relationships, as foundational trust is compromised. Individuals may become more reliant on surface-level interactions, missing opportunities to engage meaningfully with potential partners. The impact of image selection in online dating underscores the necessity for users to approach these platforms with a critical mindset. Awareness of the ways in which image curation can distort perceptions is crucial for fostering authentic connections. Encouraging profiles that include a broader representation of who individuals are—beyond physical appearances—could mitigate some of the superficial tendencies seen on these platforms. This not only fosters a more inclusive dating environment but also challenges the prevailing norms of attractiveness that dominate digital interactions. By emphasizing the importance of authenticity and personal narratives alongside images, users can shift the focus towards building meaningful relationships grounded in shared values and interests, enabling a more enriching online dating experience.

## Psychological Effects of Visual Representation

In the realm of online dating, visual representation plays a crucial role in shaping perceptions and expectations surrounding potential partners. The human brain is wired to process visual information rapidly, often leading individuals to make snap judgments based on images alone. When users create profiles adorned with carefully curated pictures, the psychological impact of these visuals can heavily influence attraction and interest. This phenomenon underscores the significance of aesthetics in the digital dating landscape, where the appeal of a profile can outweigh substantive qualities like personality or values. Consequently, while a visually appealing photo may spark initial interest, it can also create unrealistic benchmarks for physical attractiveness that can skew a users judgment, leading them to overlook deeper, more meaningful connections that go beyond superficial appearances. The consequences of relying on visual representation in online dating can lead to varying psychological effects, particularly around self-esteem and body image. Users who invest time in carefully crafting their profiles often experience anxiety over how they are perceived by others. The pressure to present an idealized version of oneself can exacerbate feelings of inadequacy, especially when confronting the seemingly perfect lives portrayed by others. This social comparison may lead to a cycle of dissatisfaction, where individuals seek validation through likes and matches, reinforcing the notion that self-worth is tethered to external acceptance. For many, this can lead to mental health challenges, as the quest for connection becomes intertwined with the harsh realities of self-image, prompting a reevaluation of what constitutes real intimacy in the context of digital relationships. The implications of visual representation extend beyond individual psychology to influence broader societal norms around dating and relationships. The emphasis on physical appearance fosters a culture of superficiality, where metrics of worthiness and desirability can be quantified by algorithms that prioritize visual attributes over emotional compatibility or shared values. This shift has not only altered traditional dating dynamics but also perpetuated stereotypes around romance and attraction. As users navigate these platforms, they may unconsciously adopt narrow criteria for partnership that reflect societal beauty standards, equating them with personal value. The result is a paradox where meaningful connections are often overshadowed by an incessant focus on visual appeal, entrenching beliefs that love can be optimized through algorithmic matching rather than genuine human connection. Understanding these psychological ramifications can empower users to approach online dating with a more critical mindset, fostering deeper, more authentic relationships amidst the visual noise.

# Case Studies on Photo Misrepresentation

Misrepresentation can take many forms in the context of online dating, particularly through photographic depictions meant to represent users authentically. A prevalent case in point involves the phenomenon of catfishing, where individuals use altered or entirely fabricated images to create deceptive profiles. One notable example is the 2010 case of a woman who posed as a model using stolen photographs from an Instagram influencer. This misrepresentation not only shattered the trust of those she corresponded with but also highlighted the psychological impacts on victims, who often find themselves grappling with self-doubt and insecurity when aligned against an idealized version of beauty or success. This manipulation of one's visual identity illustrates a broader trend within online dating: how individuals shape narratives about themselves to meet perceived societal standards or attract attention, often at the expense of honesty and genuine connection. Thus, the repercussions extend beyond individual relationships, influencing broader trends in how love and attraction are conceptualized in digital spaces. Drawing on research from the Pew Research Center, statistics reveal a significant percentage of online daters report encountering profile pictures that do not accurately represent the individual. Many individuals resort to using filters or dating app features that enhance attractiveness, intentionally skewing perceptions. This purposeful alteration of images not only complicates the initial attraction process but also sets unrealistic expectations for the eventual in-person meeting. A study indicated that nearly 50% of participants felt disappointed during their first encounters because the individuals they met looked markedly different from their online profiles. Such discrepancies can lead to a feeling of betrayal, with the initial excitement of potential love morphing into disillusionment. These encounters serve to reinforce the idea that an authentic representation is crucial for building meaningful interactions, yet superficial judgments based on pictures continue to dominate the dating landscape, perpetuating a cycle of unfulfilled expectations. Although the prevalence of misrepresentation underscores challenges in online dating, some argue that photo deception is a reflection of deeper societal pressures rather than mere individual faults. The emphasis on physical appearance in a culture steeped in visual media promotes an environment where users feel compelled to embellish their profiles to meet unfair beauty standards or societal norms. In many cases, this behavior stems from the unique nuances of online interaction, where the relative anonymity allows individuals to craft personas that may not align with their real-world identities. Thus, while misrepresentation can jeopardize the integrity of online dating processes, it also serves as a mirror reflecting the often unrealistic expectations society imposes on individuals regarding beauty and desirability. Recognizing this dynamic is critical for users seeking genuine connections, as it encourages a deeper examination of their motivations for using these platforms, urging a more authentic approach amidst a landscape temptingly optimized for superficiality.

# VIII. MYTH: ONLINE DATING IS INSTANTANEOUS

Many users entering the realm of online dating are lured by the notion of immediacy, believing that with a few swipes or clicks, they can effortlessly engage with potential partners. This perception often overlooks the complexities of human relationships that cannot be compressed into simplistic interactions. Individuals may find themselves inundated with profiles that do not lead to genuine connections. Studies illustrate that while a match may occur within seconds, the time taken to establish meaningful communication often extends far beyond that initial encounter. The digital landscape can foster superficial engagements, leading individuals to jump from one connection to another without investing the necessary emotional labor that true relationships require. Rather than yielding instant gratification, online dating frequently demands patience and a willingness to sift through numerous interactions to find compatibility. In addition to the time and emotional investment required, the expectation of instant outcomes can foster unrealistic standards that complicate the dating experience. Unlike traditional meeting methods, where individuals may organically forge connections based on shared environments and mutual acquaintances, online platforms often create environments ripe for misunderstanding. Profiles curated to attract attention may present idealized versions of self, leading to mismatches when individuals finally meet face-to-face. The anxiety surrounding immediate responses and the pressure to maintain an online presence can exacerbate feelings of inadequacy when engagements fail to align with expectations. Those who perceive online interactions as instantaneous may shy away from the more gradual process of getting to know someone deeply, ultimately undermining the potential for lasting relationships. As a result, the likelihood of genuine compatibility diminishes when users prioritize speed over substance. The narrative that online dating guarantees swift connections can obscure the underlying reality that meaningful relationships require time and effort, regardless of the platform. Each interaction, whether through text or video call, serves as a step toward understanding anothers values and aspirations. Users who treat these engagements with the patience and attention they deserve are more likely to navigate the complexities of digital romance successfully. Gradually cultivating relationships allows individuals to share their stories and establish trust, which is essential for any lasting bond. While online dating can serve as a tool for broadening ones pool of potential partners, the myth of instant connections should be dispelled in favor of a more measured approach that acknowledges the inherent challenges of building authentic relationships. Embracing this perspective not only enhances the experience of online dating but also encourages users to engage more meaningfully with their quest for connection.

## The Illusion of Quick Matches

The allure of instant gratification pervades the online dating scene, where users are often seduced by the idea of finding romance with minimal effort. This expectation, fueled by the design of many dating apps, leads individuals to believe that love is just one quick match away. In reality, the algorithms used by these platforms primarily focus on physical attraction and surface-level compatibility rather than deeper emotional or intellectual connections. This superficial approach can create an illusion of abundance, encouraging users to swipe right on numerous profiles in a choice overload scenario. While this might foster an initial sense of excitement, it often undermines the potential for meaningful relationships as genuine compatibility requires sufficient time and personal investment that a quick match cannot provide. The nature of online interactions inherently discourages the development of emotional intimacy, as many individuals prioritize immediate responses over thoughtful engagement. The pressure to maintain constant connectivity and quick replies can lead to relationships characterized more by their expediency than by authenticity. As a result, users may find themselves entangled in a series of fleeting encounters rather than cultivating lasting bonds. Studies have shown that relationships formed through traditional means often benefit from deeper roots, as they involve gradual understanding and shared experiences that foster trust and commitment. In contrast, the rapid-fire interactions typical of dating apps often breed frustration and disappointment, contributing to a cycle of short-lived romances where both parties remain elusive and unattached. The perception that online dating facilitates easy and quick matches can skew individuals understanding of romance itself. With countless profiles to explore, users may become fixated on the pursuit rather than the reality of building a relationship. This shift in focus can lead to chronic dissatisfaction, as the next best thing is always just one swipe away. It is vital to recognize that love, whether sought online or offline, is a nuanced journey that demands time, patience, and effort. The myth of quick matches can deter individuals from investing in their dating experiences, ultimately preventing them from achieving the deeper connections they seek. By reevaluating their approach and fostering more meaningful interactions, users can cultivate a healthier understanding of love in the digital age, moving beyond the superficial allure of immediate results.

## Time Investment in Online Dating

In the contemporary landscape of romance, the amount of time invested in online dating significantly impacts the success and satisfaction of users. As individuals sift through countless profiles and engage in conversations, the sheer volume of time spent can lead to diminishing returns. Many users often underestimate the commitment required to foster meaningful connections, resulting in frustration when their expectations of instant gratification are unmet. Research indicates that individuals who dedicate substantial time to engaging with potential partners – whether through messaging, video chats, or in-person meetups – report higher levels of relationship satisfaction. This time investment not only enhances the chances of forging deeper emotional connections but also aids in filtering out mismatches that may arise from impulsively swiping left or right. Those who approach online dating as a process requiring patience and effort are more likely to find lasting love. Nevertheless, the paradox of choice plays a significant role in the online dating experience, complicating the time investment aspect. The abundance of options available can overwhelm users, leading to decision fatigue and a hesitance to commit. With numerous potential matches at their fingertips, individuals may fall prey to the notion that a better option is always just a click away, making it difficult to focus on cultivating existing connections. This phenomenon not only affects the interpersonal dynamics of budding relationships but also fosters a culture of superficial interactions rooted in transient connections. Consequently, many users find themselves stuck in a cycle of short-lived encounters rather than building sustainable partnerships. By acknowledging the implications of this paradox and the time spent seeking endlessly for the "ideal" match, individuals can aim for quality over quantity, ultimately leading to more fulfilling dating experiences. The time investment in online dating can serve as a tool for personal growth and self-discovery, which is often overlooked. Users are frequently exposed to diverse perspectives and relationship styles, prompting reflection on their own desires and values. Engaging in conversations with various individuals allows people to articulate their goals and boundaries within the context of romantic relationships, fostering emotional intelligence and communication skills. This self-exploration can lead to healthier relationship patterns, as users become more attuned to their needs and those of potential partners. It is crucial that individuals recognize the difference between productive time investment and time wasted on vague interactions that yield little fulfillment. By being deliberate about their engagements and understanding the transformative potential of this journey, users can navigate the complexities of online dating more effectively, paving the way for more meaningful and enduring connections.

## The Reality of Building Relationships

Navigating the complexities of human connection in the digital age has led to a paradox in the way relationships are formed. While online platforms promise quick matches based on compatibility algorithms, the very nature of digital interactions can detract from genuine connection. Building a meaningful relationship requires more than just shared interests or appealing photos; it demands emotional vulnerability, patience, and consistent communication. In a realm where swiping left or right seems to dictate potential partners, the depth of character often gets overshadowed by superficial judgments. Research has shown that couples who meet online often face unique challenges, such as managing unrealistic expectations and a lack of authentic experiences typical of traditional dating. The reality is that relationships require effort and understanding beyond an initial attraction facilitated by a screen. The reliance on curated profiles can often lead to a distorted reality, where users project idealized versions of themselves to attract others. This can stifle genuine interactions and foster an environment of mistrust, as partners begin questioning the authenticity of their connection. Studies indicate that many individuals struggle with feelings of inadequacy or imposter syndrome when engaging in digital dating, which further complicates emotional intimacy. This phenomenon emphasizes the importance of approaching online dating with a realistic mindset, acknowledging that the façade presented in profiles should not be regarded as the totality of a person's character. Genuine relationships flourish in environments that encourage open dialogue, thereby allowing individuals to peel back layers of carefully constructed personas. Establishing a foundation built on honesty and authenticity is essential for transitioning from initial encounters to deeper connections. The quest for love amidst the digital noise underscores a critical evolution in societal norms regarding relationships. While technology has broadened access to potential partners, it has simultaneously heightened the challenge of discerning true compatibility from fleeting attraction. The seduction of instant gratification can lead to rushed decisions, often at the expense of meaningful, long-term relationships. To counter this trend, individuals need to engage more thoughtfully with online platforms, setting intentional boundaries and fostering patience in the process. By prioritizing quality interactions over quantity, users can cultivate connections that may eventually navigate the complexities of modern relationships. Recognizing that true love is not merely a product of algorithms but a collective journey of discovery and growth is vital. This awareness can transform online dating from a superficial experience into a genuinely enriching personal journey toward connection and understanding.

# IX. TRUTH: ALGORITHMS SHAPE OUR MATCHES

In the realm of online dating, the use of algorithms has significantly transformed how individuals are connected, often leading to unexpected outcomes. These algorithms analyze user behavior, preferences, and demographic information to create profiles that match users with potential partners, yet they often prioritize superficial traits over deeper compatibility factors. While a user may find profiles that visually appeal to them, the underlying emotional and psychological profiles remain underexplored. This tendency raises critical questions about whether such connections, often dictated by curated data, genuinely reflect the complexities of human relationships. Algorithms tend to reinforce existing biases, leading to matched preferences that may not extend beyond a narrow spectrum of characteristics. While algorithms offer efficiency in navigating the vast pool of potential partners, they also risk oversimplifying individuals and devaluing nuanced emotional connections. The reality of algorithmic matchmaking becomes even more complex when one considers the potential for misinformation within user-generated profiles. The prevalence of curated self-presentation encourages individuals to highlight the best aspects of themselves, potentially creating a dissonance between real-life interactions and online personas. Studies show that many users intentionally misrepresent their interests, lifestyles, or even physical appearances to align better with perceived preferences in their desired matches. This phenomenon not only compromises the integrity of personal connections but also fosters an environment where trust becomes a precious commodity. As users engage with a filtered version of potential partners, the authenticity of relationships can suffer, leading to disillusionment and frustration when the realities of compatibility clash with the algorithms projections. The disconnection between user intentions and algorithmic representations complicates the pursuit of genuine connection in the digital landscape. As users navigate the evolving terrain of online dating, understanding the manipulative undercurrents of technology is essential for establishing meaningful relationships. By recognizing that their matches are primarily shaped by algorithmic processes, individuals can approach these platforms with a more discerning mindset. Awareness of the limitations of algorithms can empower users to engage more authentically within the online space, seeking self-awareness and honesty in both profile creation and interpersonal interactions. Establishing clear personal goals and being mindful of the curated nature of online portrayals can help redefine users expectations from these platforms. As romantic connections continue to be navigated through the lens of technology, leveraging the benefits of online dating while remaining aware of its inherent challenges can foster a healthier and more realistic understanding of modern love. Consequently, these insights serve not only to enhance personal experiences but also contribute to a broader discourse on the impact of technology on human relationships.

## How Dating Algorithms Work

Propelled by advancements in data science, modern dating algorithms analyze user behavior and preferences to optimize matchmaking processes. These algorithms function primarily through machine learning, where they continuously adapt and improve based on accumulated data. Initially, users provide personal information and answers to survey questions related to their interests and values. This input forms the baseline for creating a user profile, while the algorithm simultaneously tracks interactions—such as swipes or messages—to gauge what types of connections users favor. The computational models then cross-reference this data with those of other users, factoring in variables like geographical proximity, shared interests, and compatibility scores. Thus, the algorithms not only strive to deliver potential matches but also align with user behaviors and engagement levels, enhancing the chances for successful connections, often in real-time as they learn and adjust to new data points. The effectiveness of these algorithms can sometimes create an illusion of perfect compatibility, leading users to harbor unrealistic expectations about their dating experiences. Users may equate the frequency of matches with the potential for meaningful relationships, yet the curated lists generated by algorithms often lack the qualitative nuances that define deep personal connections. As a result, individuals may find themselves overwhelmed by an array of options, fostering superficial judgments based solely on visual appeal or minimal text. The reliance on algorithms underscores a paradox in digital dating; while they offer efficiency in finding potential partners, they may inadvertently promote a culture of disposability. This binary decision-making through swiping mechanisms could lead to a diminishing sense of emotional investment, as users may fall into habitual patterns of engagement rather than forming substantive connections. Critics of dating algorithms argue that the reliance on metrics and data can lead to homogenized experiences, disregarding the myriad factors that contribute to human attraction and bonding. While these models claim to optimize matchmaking, they may inadvertently reinforce existing biases by prioritizing certain characteristics over others. Dating platforms may favor profiles that fit conventional attractiveness standards or highlight users educational backgrounds, neglecting the depth of personality traits that truly foster romance. Research indicates that users often feel frustrated by seemingly limitless options, leading to what psychologists term choice overload, where the abundance of potential matches discourages commitment. Consequently, while algorithms can serve as tools for convenience, they also risk oversimplifying the complex nature of human relationships, necessitating a more nuanced understanding of love in the digital realm.

## The Influence of Data on Compatibility

Algorithm-driven matchmaking has fundamentally reshaped the landscape of online dating, offering users a streamlined approach to finding potential partners. This technology leverages vast amounts of data to identify patterns in user behavior, preferences, and interactions, ultimately influencing the compatibility assessments it makes. While this might suggest a more scientific approach to love, it raises critical questions about the depth and quality of these connections. Many dating platforms utilize personality quizzes and user-generated interests to create profiles that, theoretically, enhance compatibility. The efficacy of these algorithms depends heavily on the quality and accuracy of the data entered by users, leading to a paradox where the pursuit of a perfect match may hinge on incomplete or even misleading information. Thus, while data can serve as a valuable tool in the quest for love, it is essential to recognize its limitations and the risk of fostering superficial connections. The allure of digital matchmaking often overshadows the subtleties of human relationships, resulting in a skewed perception of compatibility. As users engage with platforms promising algorithmically curated matches, they may overlook the immensely complex nature of human emotions and interpersonal dynamics. A myriad of factors—such as cultural backgrounds, life experiences, and individual values—play crucial roles in fostering deep connections that algorithms may fail to account for. The emphasis on immediate outcomes and statistics, such as swipe counts or message response rates, can diminish users appreciation for the gradual process of developing meaningful relationships. Consequently, while data-driven compatibility can facilitate introductions, it must be accompanied by an understanding of the intricacies of genuine connection. Users may find themselves at risk of prioritizing efficiency over authenticity, potentially leading to dissatisfaction when their experiences do not align with their lofty expectations. Engaging with online dating platforms also fosters an evolving landscape where self-presentation takes precedence over genuine connection. Many users curate profiles that may idealize or misrepresent their true selves to align with perceived compatibility metrics, thus perpetuating a cycle of dissatisfaction rooted in unrealistic portrayals. This phenomenon can significantly distort the very nature of compatibility, as individuals often fall prey to the emphasis on physical attractiveness or shared interests rather than deeper emotional connections. Users may develop a "shopping mentality," viewing potential partners as mere selections rather than individuals with unique stories and desires. As this dynamic unfolds, it becomes increasingly important to navigate the complexities of online dating with a critical lens, understanding that while data and algorithms can serve as useful tools, true compatibility is ultimately defined by the depth of emotional resonance and mutual understanding that transcends statistical measures. Approaching online dating with realistic expectations and a keen awareness of datas influence may enable individuals to cultivate sincerely meaningful connections.

## Limitations of Algorithmic Matching

The effectiveness of algorithmic matching hinges on a plethora of factors, yet it often overlooks the intricacies of human relationships, prioritizing data points over emotional connection. While dating algorithms rely heavily on user preferences, behaviors, and demographic data, they fail to capture the subtleties of personal chemistry and compatibility, which are crucial in forming meaningful relationships. Two individuals might score highly on an algorithmic compatibility scale, yet, in reality, they may find themselves unable to establish rapport or connect on a deeper emotional level. This reliance on quantitative assessment can lead users to devalue or overlook the more qualitative aspects of relationships, such as shared values, humor, or life experiences, which can significantly influence relational dynamics. Consequently, this limitation may lead to dissatisfaction when users find that their algorithmically suggested matches lack the spark necessary for lasting connections. Algorithmic matching systems often reinforce existing biases, hindering users from exploring diverse options that may foster unexpected yet enriching connections. Algorithms generally prioritize matching users based on predetermined criteria, such as race, socioeconomic status, or educational background, often perpetuating societal norms and limiting user exposure to a broader spectrum of potential partners. This tendency can result in creating echo chambers where individuals find themselves engaging only with those who share their backgrounds or viewpoints, effectively stifling opportunities for genuine connection. As dating platforms strategically utilize user data to produce highly personalized experiences, the consequence could be a problematic narrowing of choices, leading users to miss out on relationships that could challenge their perspectives and help them grow. Thus, this limitation calls for users to critically engage with the algorithms, being aware that, while they serve as a guide, those algorithms are not infallible. The phenomenon of choice overload emerges from the vast array of options that dating platforms present, which algorithmic matching only exacerbates. When individuals are bombarded with numerous potential matches, the sheer volume can lead to frustration and indecision rather than ease in the selection process. This paradox of choice can result in users feeling overwhelmed, ultimately making them less satisfied with their selections and leading to second-guessing or regret about the choices made. The overwhelming focus on quantity often detracts from meaningful engagement, prompting superficial judgments based on first impressions rather than allowing users the time to delve deeper into potential connections. This fragmented approach can hinder the discovery of genuine relationships, reinforcing a cycle of fleeting interactions over sustaining bonds. Recognizing this limitation in algorithmic matching encourages users to adopt a more selective and intentional approach, enhancing their chances for meaningful connections amidst the sea of online possibilities.

# X. MYTH: ONLINE DATING IS SAFE

In the context of online dating, the perception of safety is often misconstrued, leading many users to underestimate the potential risks involved. Although dating platforms typically implement safety features such as photos flagged for scrutiny and reporting mechanisms for inappropriate behavior, these precautions may not be sufficient to protect individuals from predatory behavior. The anonymity afforded by the internet can enable individuals with malicious intentions to misrepresent themselves easily. A significant study conducted by the Pew Research Center found that approximately 30% of online dating users reported experiences with suspicious behavior, illustrating that behind the comforting facade of a screen, real dangers lurk. The very nature of online interactions can foster a false sense of security; users may inadvertently share personal information without fully grasping the implications, leaving them vulnerable. Thus, the belief that these platforms are intrinsically safe can lead individuals to lower their guard, potentially exposing them to harmful situations. The depersonalized interaction afforded by digital communication complicates the landscape of trust and safety further. Online profiles, often curated to showcase the best versions of ourselves, can conceal critical aspects of a person's identity or intentions. Studies have demonstrated that many individuals embellish their online personas, which can lead to disillusionment when confrontations with their true self occur. This deliberate presentation of a false identity not only jeopardizes individual safety but also complicates the groundwork of trust, a crucial element in any relationship. When users project an embellished version of themselves—whether through attractive photographs or misleading descriptions—potential partners may unknowingly place their trust in someone who doesnt genuinely represent their character. Thus, while the act of finding a romantic partner online can be enticing, the superficial allure of profiles can mask deeper vulnerabilities, making the notion of safety a myth rather than a reality. The emotional ramifications of online dating risks contribute significantly to the myth of safety. Despite the convenience and expansive reach of dating apps, users may encounter significant emotional turmoil resulting from deceptive practices within these platforms. Ghosting, catfishing, and manipulation are just a few examples of how virtual interactions can lead to heartbreak and distrust that linger long after the digital connection is severed. The anonymity provided by online platforms can embolden individuals to engage in hurtful tactics that would be less likely to occur in face-to-face interactions. The immediacy of swiping and messaging can foster an environment where meaningful connections are sacrificed for fleeting interactions, leading to increased anxiety and lower self-esteem among users. As individuals increasingly rely on these platforms to fulfill their romantic aspirations, the potential for emotional harm becomes another layer in the myth of safety, emphasizing the need for users to approach online dating with cautious optimism and a critical eye.

## Risks Associated with Online Dating

Concealed identities and curated profiles undeniably form a significant part of the allure surrounding online dating. A major concern is the prevalence of dishonesty among users, as individuals often present an idealized version of themselves that can lead to mismatched expectations. Studies indicate that a substantial portion of singles on dating platforms selectively choose their photos or embellish personal traits, which can result in a deceptive environment. This disconnection between reality and the curated online persona not only can breed distrust but may lead to emotional distress when the relationship progresses. Individuals who invest time and emotional energy into these interactions may find themselves confronting the bitter realization that the individual they have formed a connection with is not entirely who they claimed to be. Such discrepancies can undermine the very foundation of trust that is essential for any relationship, especially new ones formed in the nebulous space of digital interaction. Another crucial risk associated with online dating pertains to personal safety and privacy. Users often provide sensitive information in their profiles, which can be exploited by malicious individuals. Notably, stalking and harassment have emerged as significant concerns within this context. Reports highlight instances where seemingly harmless exchanges escalated into threatening behavior, underscoring the potential dangers that lurk behind seemingly innocent introductions. The anonymity afforded by these platforms can embolden unscrupulous individuals to engage in predatory behavior. Victims may find themselves manipulated into revealing personal information, leading to scenarios such as identity theft or catfishing, where one assumes a fabricated identity to exploit others emotionally or financially. These risks emphasize the critical importance of online safety precautions, advocating for a cautious approach to sharing personal information until trust has been established more concretely. The ephemeral nature of online connections can also contribute to superficiality in relationships, often accented by the fast-paced, swipe-right culture of dating apps. This mode of courtship encourages a commodified view of relationships, reducing potential romantic partners to mere photographs and brief bios. Research suggests that this superficiality can lead to a decrease in meaningful connections, as individuals prioritize physical attraction over deeper compatibility. As a result, emotional fulfillment may be sacrificed at the altar of instant gratification. This culture of immediacy may foster a cycle of frustration, as individuals oscillate between multiple matches, often leading to decision fatigue and a diminished sense of commitment. In a society where the conversation surrounding love and relationships is becoming increasingly casual, the challenge remains to cultivate authentic connections that carry depth and longevity, pushing back against a trend that risks relegating love to a fleeting momentary exchange.

## Common Scams and Fraudulent Behavior

In the realm of online dating, individuals must remain vigilant against a variety of scams that exploit the emotional vulnerabilities of users. Romance scams, where perpetrators create fake profiles to establish fraudulent relationships, have surged in recent years. Typically, these scammers cultivate a relationship over weeks or months, employing emotional manipulation to gain trust before ultimately soliciting money for emergencies or travel expenses. This predatory behavior not only drains financial resources but also inflicts significant emotional distress on victims who may feel betrayed or humiliated. Awareness of these tactics is crucial, as many victims report feeling isolated and ashamed, which can inhibit their willingness to seek help or share their experiences. Education around the signs of romance scams is essential for empowering online daters to approach potential partners with increased skepticism and to foster a safer online dating environment. Another prevalent form of deceit involves identity theft, where scammers use stolen or fake identities to create profiles on dating platforms. These fraudulent accounts can lead to various dangers, including harassment and financial loss. Victims may unknowingly communicate with someone assuming a false identity, which can lead to situations where personal information is shared, possibly resulting in further exploitation. This behavior not only violates the trust inherent in romantic engagements but also exposes users to broader risks, such as unwanted attention or malicious behavior by those masking their true intentions. Its critical that users adopt rigorous privacy measures, such as limiting the information shared until trust is established. Online dating sites must also take responsibility by implementing robust verification systems to mitigate the prevalence of identity-related scams, thereby safeguarding the user experience while promoting authenticity in connections. The influence of algorithm-driven matchmaking also plays a significant role in fostering a culture of superficiality that can sometimes accompany online dating. While technology allows for efficient filtering of potential partners based on preferences and behaviors, it can inadvertently promote hasty judgments based on limited information—namely, photographs and brief bios. This superficiality may lead individuals to prioritize appearance over compatibility, diminishing the likelihood of forming meaningful, lasting connections. Algorithms often amplify existing biases, creating echo chambers in which users are continuously swayed toward partners that fit narrow criteria, inadvertently perpetuating skewed perceptions of desirability.

As such, it is vital for users to approach these platforms with a mindset that values depth and understanding over superficial attributes. Developers of dating apps could reevaluate the design of their algorithms to encourage more holistic interactions, thereby fostering connections that reflect authentic emotional compatibility rather than purely visual appeal.

## Importance of Safety Precautions

In the realm of online dating, the importance of implementing safety precautions cannot be overstated. Navigating the digital dating landscape involves engaging with individuals who may not be who they claim to be, raising significant concerns regarding personal safety and emotional well-being. Users must remain vigilant, adopting a proactive approach to scrutinizing profiles and communicating with potential partners. Many platforms offer built-in safety features, such as profile verification and reporting mechanisms, which can significantly enhance a users sense of security. Educating oneself about common red flags—such as inconsistent stories or avoidance of personal details—can be instrumental in preventing potentially harmful encounters. By taking these precautions, individuals not only protect themselves but also foster a safer online community for all users, allowing for a more trusting and genuine experience during these often vulnerable interactions. The adherence to safety protocols extends beyond initial interactions, playing a crucial role in the transition from online to in-person meetings. Once a level of comfort is established through digital communication, it is essential to approach face-to-face encounters with prudence. Selecting public venues for the first meetings significantly mitigates risks and ensures an environment that is conducive to open, honest dialogue. Informing friends or family about one's plans adds an extra layer of safety, as it holds individuals accountable for their whereabouts while providing an additional safety net. These measures not only safeguard against potential risks but also allow individuals to focus on the interaction itself, enhancing the likelihood of genuine connections. By prioritizing safety, users empower themselves to make informed decisions, allowing the digital dating experience to unfold in a manner that is both enjoyable and secure. A conscious approach to safety can fundamentally transform the online dating experience, steering it towards a more fulfilling pursuit of genuine relationships. Many myths surrounding digital dating perpetuate the notion that love can be effortlessly obtained through mere clicks, overlooking the nuances involved in human connection. By exercising caution and maintaining realistic expectations, users are positioned to navigate the often overwhelming array of choices more thoughtfully. Integrating safety measures as a core component of the online dating strategy can help individuals discern between authentic potential partners and misleading profiles. Consequently, this awareness not only mitigates potential dangers but also enriches the dating experience, offering opportunities for meaningful interactions grounded in trust and mutual respect. Emphasizing safety serves as a foundation for engaging with online platforms purposefully and responsibly, ultimately benefiting those seeking companionship in this increasingly digital world.

# XI. TRUTH: COMMUNICATION STYLES VARY

Effective communication is fundamental in forging authentic connections, especially in the realm of online dating, where the nuances of interpersonal interaction can be easily lost. People often express their personalities through various communication styles, which can dramatically influence their online dating experience. Some users prefer to engage in playful banter, using humor to diffuse the initial awkwardness, while others may adopt a more serious tone, seeking deeper, more meaningful conversations right from the start. These differences can lead to misunderstandings; what one person perceives as flirtation might be interpreted by another as insincerity. This divergence in styles not only affects individual interactions but can also skew users perceptions of themselves and their potential partners. Hence, recognizing these variations is crucial for navigating the online dating landscape effectively, as it allows individuals to adapt their approaches and establish more genuine connections. As algorithms increasingly mediate our interactions, they impact communication styles by filtering and prioritizing how we engage with potential matches. Many dating platforms utilize data-driven algorithms that categorize users based on shared interests and personality traits, which can inadvertently lead to superficial interactions. When profiles are condensed to a few images and brief descriptions, the depth of communication is often sacrificed, leaving users to rely heavily on first impressions rather than substantive discussions. This algorithmic influence can perpetuate a cycle of exchanging shallow messages, where individuals present curated versions of themselves, sometimes leading to disillusionment when actual in-person interactions reveal discrepancies between online personas and reality. Recognizing the role of these algorithms prompts a more critical assessment of the dating experience, highlighting the importance of fostering open communication that transcends the superficial boundaries set by technology. Navigating different communication styles also raises awareness of the inherent complexities within interpersonal relationships shaped by online platforms. While some individuals thrive in quick, text-based exchanges, preferring concise interactions over lengthy dialogues, others may yearn for deeper emotional connections that require more robust communication. The challenge, then, is to strike a balance between the immediacy of digital conversations and the intricate tapestry of human emotions. Users must become attuned to their communication preferences and those of others to cultivate genuine connections. This awareness can lead to richer interactions, wherein individuals feel encouraged to share their authentic selves rather than presenting idealized versions. By embracing the diversity of communication styles and actively engaging in meaningful dialogues, online daters can unlock the potential for true connection, moving beyond myths of instantaneous love to embrace a more nuanced understanding of relationships in the digital age.

## Differences in Online vs. Offline Communication

The dynamics of communication in the digital age diverge significantly from traditional interpersonal interactions. In online communication, the lack of physical presence often alters the nuances and subtleties that characterize face-to-face exchanges. The absence of nonverbal cues—such as body language, facial expressions, and tone of voice—can lead to misunderstandings and misinterpretations. This limitation is particularly pronounced in the realm of online dating, where individuals are confined to curated profiles and scripted messages. The thrill of real-time dialogue, with its spontaneous reactions and emotional depth, is often lost in a digital context, potentially reducing the richness of connection. Thus, while the online arena offers an expansive reach across geographic boundaries, it simultaneously risks fostering superficial interactions that may lack the foundational elements of genuine human bonding. The erosion of these nuances raises critical questions about the authenticity of relationships formed through digital platforms. Through the lens of immediacy, online communication presents both opportunities and challenges in the pursuit of romantic connection. The instant gratification associated with messaging apps and dating websites can create a paradox; while these tools enable rapid exchanges and quick accessibility, they can also lead to a culture of disposability. Users may find themselves scrolling through profiles and swiping left or right, treating potential partners more like products than people. This behavior reflects a broader societal trend where technology facilitates impulsivity and superficiality, impacting the quality of romantic engagements. Offline interactions, by contrast, often foster a more deliberate and contemplative process of getting to know someone. Engaging in conversation or shared activities in physical spaces allows for relational depth that can be obscured in online settings. This juxtaposition highlights the importance of understanding how the mechanisms of both forms of communication shape emotional connections and the potential longevity of relationships initiated in these environments. The prominence of digital dating platforms underscores significant shifts in relationship-building strategies, particularly among younger demographics. The allure of algorithm-driven matchmaking can lead individuals to prioritize compatibility indicators, such as interests and lifestyle choices, based primarily on profiles presented on screens. This reliance on quantifiable data may overlook the critical importance of emotional resonance, which often flourishes in organic settings of engagement. In stark contrast, offline relationships evolve through shared experiences, layers of interaction, and natural emotional growth. This divergence suggests a need for a more nuanced perspective on how online dating shapes the modern conception of love. Establishing an awareness of these differing forms of communication can empower individuals to navigate the online dating landscape with a more discerning eye. By recognizing the advantages and limitations of both online and offline modalities, users may become more adept at forging meaningful connections that transcend the superficial nature of digital encounters, ultimately leading to more fulfilling romantic relationships.

## The Role of Texting in Modern Dating

In contemporary dating, the evolution of communication has transformed the way people initiate and nurture relationships. Texting has emerged as a primary mode of interaction, bridging distances and allowing for a quicker exchange of thoughts and feelings. This immediacy can both enhance and hinder romantic pursuits; while it offers an opportunity for rapid connection, it often lacks the depth and nuance that face-to-face communication provides. Research indicates that many individuals rely on texting to gauge compatibility, leading to a superficial assessment of potential partners. Texting fosters a culture of immediacy, where responses are expected swiftly, creating pressure that can complicate relationship dynamics. This reliance on text-based communication can certainly expedite conversations, but it may inadvertently cultivate misunderstandings or misinterpretations, as tone and emotion are frequently lost in digital conversation. Texting plays a significant role in setting the rhythm of modern romance, allowing for a gradual revelation of intimacy without the pressures of traditional dating encounters. Unlike the past, where individuals might guard their feelings until an in-person meeting, couples today often share personal stories and aspirations through their devices. This can be a double-edged sword; while emotional sharing can strengthen bonds, it may also lead to premature intimacy, where partners reveal too much too soon. The phenomenon of texting after a date serves as a litmus test for interest, with eager anticipation surrounding responses. If one partner delays or avoids replying, it can provoke anxiety and doubt, skewing perceptions of the relationships potential. In this context, the voluminous exchanges common in texting can foster not just connection but also insecurity, as expectations surrounding communication frequency evolve rapidly among younger generations. The impact of texting on modern dating extends to its influence on self-presentation and identity management. Individuals often curate their messages and profiles to reflect the idealized versions of themselves, which can lead to a disconnect between digital personas and real-life identities. This phenomenon solidifies the notion of performance in dating, where every text is a calculated move in the continuing game of attraction. The rise of texting as the dominant form of communication may also reduce the likelihood of encountering potential partners in genuine, serendipitous situations, further entrenching users in a cycle of digital interaction. Texting may amplify existing biases and misapprehensions, creating an environment where individuals are less likely to pursue deeper connections. As technology continues to shape the dating landscape, individuals must navigate these complexities, striving for authenticity amidst the allure of curated online communication. Balancing textual exchanges with traditional interactions may hold the key to forming meaningful relationships in the digital era.

## Misinterpretations in Digital Communication

In the realm of digital communication, the nuances of interpretation are often lost, leading to miscommunications that can derail budding relationships. Text-based interactions, devoid of vocal tone and body language, leave a significant gap in conveying intentions and emotions. A simple message can be perceived as sarcastic when intended to be playful, or overly blunt when meant to be straightforward. These misinterpretations can foster misunderstandings that escalate into conflict, making it crucial for individuals to develop a keen awareness of the limitations inherent in digital communication. As users navigate these platforms, they may also misjudge the gravity of their words, believing that a breezy, casual approach suffices when expressing deeper feelings. This tendency can ultimately undermine the potential for forming genuine emotional connections, transforming what might have been a budding romance into an exchange of frustration and confusion. Anticipating how messages are received by others requires active listening—or, in the digital context, active reading. The absence of nonverbal cues compels individuals to rely heavily on context, including past interactions and personal biases, to infer meaning. Consequently, one person's benign comment may be interpreted as an insult by another, clouded by insecurities or preconceived notions. The layered meanings that messages can carry vary widely across different demographic groups and cultural backgrounds, compounding the challenge of proper interpretation. What one community views as light-hearted banter may be seen as offensive by another. Thus, the rich tapestry of human communication is often reduced to mere words on a screen, sacrificing the depth of understanding that face-to-face interaction provides. To mitigate these risks, users must cultivate empathy and patience, recognizing the inherent imperfections of written communication and allowing space for clarifications in their online exchanges. The allure of digital platforms often leads individuals to curate their online personas, adding another layer of complexity to communication. Profiles are constructed not just as depictions of individuals but as strategic presentations designed to attract potential partners. This curation can lead to a significant dissonance between the self that individuals present online and the reality of their lives, further complicating interactions. Someone might post a picture from a particularly flattering angle or highlight certain interests while downplaying quirks that might be less appealing. These selective presentations can create unrealistic expectations and an environment ripe for misinterpretation when messages begin to flow. As users engage with richly edited portrayals of each other, the line between authentic attraction and superficial interest blurs. While digital platforms enhance the ability to connect, they simultaneously challenge the fundamental aspects of honest communication and genuine understanding, leaving relationships vulnerable to the very misinterpretations that could have been avoided through more direct interaction.

# XII. MYTH: ONLINE DATING IS FOR YOUNG PEOPLE

While many associate online dating with the younger generation, a growing demographic of older individuals is increasingly turning to digital platforms to find companionship. In fact, research indicates that nearly 35% of online dating users are over the age of 50, significantly challenging the stereotype that online dating is exclusively for the young. This trend can be attributed to several factors, including the decline of traditional social structures, such as communities and friendships, which once provided avenues for meeting potential partners. Technology has become remarkably user-friendly, reducing the apprehension older individuals often feel when engaging with digital platforms. Many seniors are discovering the vast potential of these sites, not only as a means to meet romantic interests but also as an opportunity to expand their social circles. As a result, the notion that online dating is limited to the youth overlooks the diverse user base actively participating in these modern matchmaking methods. Age-appropriate online dating sites are emerging to cater specifically to older adults, thereby fostering a sense of community and understanding among users. Numerous platforms now focus on the needs of those over 50, offering features designed to address the unique concerns of this age group, such as flexibility in communication styles and options for serious relationships. These websites create safe spaces for older daters to share experiences and offer support, which is especially important as they navigate what can be a daunting transition into dating later in life. Studies show that older users often approach online dating with a more mature perspective, looking for meaningful connections rather than the casual flings that often attract younger individuals. This maturity allows them to cultivate relationships built on shared values and mutual respect, reinforcing the idea that online dating can cater to all stages of life. In debunking the myth that online dating is solely for the young, it becomes clear that numerous societal shifts and technological advancements have transformed the landscape of romantic connections. By embracing the digital dating world, older individuals are not simply trying to replicate the dating experiences of their youth; they are exploring new avenues for love and companionship aligned with their current lifestyles. The greater acceptance of technology among various age groups highlights the versatility of online dating platforms, enabling individuals of any age to engage with potential partners in meaningful ways. As more seniors join these platforms, the stigma surrounding older individuals using online dating continues to diminish, paving the way for a broader acceptance of diverse dating practices. Consequently, understanding the true demographics of online dating becomes essential for dismantling outdated perceptions and promoting a more inclusive view of modern romance.

## Age Demographics in Online Dating

The diverse age demographics participating in online dating reveal significant insights into the motivations and behaviors associated with this contemporary pursuit of romance. Millennials, for instance, account for a substantial portion of users on dating platforms, primarily drawn to the convenience and accessibility that these services provide. Their proficiency with technology and social media plays a crucial role in shaping how they engage with potential partners. As the first generation to grow up with the internet, millennials often seek instant gratification and connections that reflect their busy lifestyles. In contrast, older generations—such as Gen X and Baby Boomers—may adopt online dating out of necessity rather than preference, often viewing it as a means to overcome loneliness or as a supplement to traditional dating methods. This disparity highlights a range of factors, including technological fluency, social habits, and relational aspirations, which together create a complex tapestry of online dating behavior across different age groups. The impact of age demographics on online dating platforms extends beyond user motivations; it also influences the design and functionality of these sites. Many dating platforms strategically cater to specific age brackets by tailoring features and user experiences accordingly. Apps targeting younger audiences often emphasize swiping mechanics and visual appeal, capitalizing on the immediacy that younger users desire. Conversely, those aimed at older individuals tend to prioritize user-friendly interfaces and detailed profiles, fostering deeper connections through comprehensive personal narratives. This tailored approach not only affects user engagement but also shapes the perceptions of what dating should entail in different age groups. Older users may face unique challenges, such as navigating the nuances of digital communication and potentially encountering generational biases within the online dating landscape, which can further exacerbate feelings of isolation or frustration. Understanding age demographics in online dating is essential for unpacking the broader implications of how love is pursued in the digital era. The intersection between age and dating behavior reveals that different generations possess distinct relational goals, comfort levels with technology, and expectations from romantic encounters. Consequently, these differences underscore a critical need for platforms to foster inclusivity and adaptability, ensuring that users of all ages find meaningful connections without succumbing to the pressures of superficial engagements. Awareness concerning these demographic nuances allows for a more nuanced discussion around the advantages and challenges inherent in online dating. As society continues to evolve, the strategies employed in digital dating must also reflect an evolving understanding of love, relationships, and the myriad ways people seek them, ensuring that platforms serve as genuine facilitators of connection rather than mere transactional environments.

## Trends Among Older Daters

The landscape of online dating has evolved significantly to accommodate the unique preferences and needs of older individuals entering the dating scene. As people age, their motivations for dating often shift, prioritizing companionship, emotional connection, and shared experiences over casual encounters. This demographic increasingly favors platforms tailored specifically for seniors, such as OurTime and SilverSingles, which cater to their desire for more meaningful relationships rather than fleeting connections. The gradual acceptance of technology among older adults has led to increased participation in online dating, as they recognize the convenience and potential it offers to meet new people. This influx into online spaces has also prompted many dating sites to adapt their user interfaces to ensure they are accessible, fostering a more inclusive environment that empowers older daters to navigate the digital landscape with confidence. Shifting social norms around aging have also contributed to the changing dynamics among older daters. Unlike previous generations, who may have retreated from the dating scene post-retirement, today's seniors often embrace their single status and seek to enjoy the dating life anew. The normalization of dating at an older age has led to a decrease in stigma, allowing individuals to explore relationships freely regardless of prior marital status or age-related stereotypes. Data collected from surveys indicate that many older daters are now more open to unconventional relationship structures, including casual dating and companionship, leading to an increase in diverse relationship models. This shift reflects broader societal trends that challenge traditional views on love and partnership, encouraging older adults to pursue happiness on their own terms, embracing the variety of connection possibilities available through digital platforms. Despite the advantages of online dating, older daters must navigate specific challenges that may complicate their experiences. One prominent issue is the prevalence of deceptive profiles, a concern that resonates deeply within this age group, who may be less familiar with the nuanced online behaviors that younger generations tend to better navigate. The potential for misrepresentation—in terms of age, appearance, or intentions—can lead to disillusionment and distrust among older users. The fear of online scams or fraud presents an additional hurdle, making older daters more cautious in their interactions. To mitigate these risks, it is essential for older adults to educate themselves on identifying red flags and practicing online safety. Enhancing users' awareness and knowledge of digital dating environments can empower them to engage more confidently, ultimately leading to richer and more satisfying connections in their pursuit of love in this critical stage of life.

## The Appeal of Online Dating Across Ages

Across various age groups, online dating platforms have become increasingly integrated into the social fabric of modern romance. For younger users, these platforms offer an accessible means of meeting new people outside their immediate social circles. The prevalence of smartphones and social media has normalized the concept of virtual connections, making dating apps an attractive option for college students and young professionals. This demographic often desires instant gratification and immediate social interaction, which online dating conveniently provides. Meanwhile, older generations, including singles in their 40s and above, are also finding significant success in the online dating realm. For those who may have faced challenges re-entering the dating scene after a long-term relationship or divorce, these platforms offer a welcoming environment to foster connections where traditional dating avenues may have faltered. The appeal of online dating spans beyond mere convenience; it represents a shift in societal norms regarding love and relationships. Traditional dating often relied on geography and mutual acquaintances, limiting options and opportunities. Platforms harness advanced algorithms and geographic data to widen the pool of potential matches, making it possible for users to connect with individuals they would likely never encounter in everyday life. This digital approach allows users to refine their search according to personal preferences and traits, fostering a sense of agency in the dating process. Consequently, this aligns with the broader cultural trend towards individualism, where personal choice becomes paramount. Yet, while increased options can be beneficial, they also pose challenges, such as decision fatigue and the paradox of choice, where the abundance of options may lead to dissatisfaction with available matches. Throughout different life stages, the motivations for engaging with online dating sites also evolve. Younger users often seek casual relationships and social engagement, driven by a culture that embraces exploration and flexibility. Conversely, older individuals may come to these platforms with more defined goals, including the desire for serious, long-term relationships. This divergence in aspirations can lead to potential mismatches in expectations, complicating interactions between age groups. The portrayal of individuals on these platforms often relies heavily on visual impressions, frequently leading to superficial assessments based on profile photos and bios, regardless of the users age. This superficiality raises critical questions about the underlying intentions and authenticity of connections. As online dating continues to grow in popularity, it becomes essential for users to navigate these platforms thoughtfully, balancing the quest for companionship with an understanding of the potential pitfalls.

# XIII. TRUTH: ONLINE DATING CAN BE EMOTIONALLY CHALLENGING

Navigating the landscape of online dating can seem both exhilarating and daunting, particularly when one delves into the emotional ramifications involved. Although platforms promise myriad potential matches, users often find themselves grappling with the reality of disconnection and frustration. Many individuals may experience the paradox of choice, where the sheer volume of options leads to decision fatigue, ultimately causing anxiety rather than enhancing satisfaction. As users swipe through profiles seeking a meaningful connection, they frequently confront the ephemeral nature of interactions, which can foster a sense of inadequacy or rejection when connections fail to materialize. This emotional toll becomes especially pronounced for those who invest significant time and hope into forming relationships, only to encounter superficial engagements that leave them feeling unfulfilled. The tendency to curate idealized online personas complicates the pursuit of genuine emotional connections. Profiles often showcase carefully selected images and descriptions, presenting a polished version of oneself that may not accurately reflect reality. This gap between expectation and reality can lead to disillusionment, especially when users are met with contrasting behaviors or appearances during the first in-person meetings. Research indicates that the phenomenon of catfishing—where users assume deceptive identities—exacerbates feelings of betrayal and distrust within the online dating community. Such experiences may not only discourage individuals from continuing their search but can also instigate deeper emotional challenges, including anxiety and lowered self-esteem, as they navigate a landscape laden with dishonesty and facade. The cumulative effect of these emotional challenges can skew individuals perceptions of love and intimacy, leading to a more superficial understanding of relationships. As individuals increasingly rely on quick assessments and virtual interactions, they may overlook the deeper qualities that foster genuine connections. Studies reveal that this trend reflects a broader cultural shift toward immediacy and convenience, often at the expense of emotional depth and relational satisfaction. Consequently, users may enter romantic entanglements with unattainable expectations, believing that ideal partnerships are readily available with a mere swipe. This mindset not only distorts the reality of dating but can also reinforce a cycle of disappointment and disengagement, ultimately hindering one's ability to cultivate meaningful romantic connections. Recognizing the emotional complexities inherent in online dating is vital for users navigating this modern landscape.

## The Impact of Rejection

Experiencing rejection can significantly shape an individuals emotional landscape, influencing self-esteem and perceptions of self-worth. Online dating amplifies this phenomenon, particularly as users engage with potential partners through profiles that often present idealized versions of reality. When the anticipation of a meaningful connection is met with negation, the psychological impact can be pronounced. Research has shown that repeated exposure to rejection, often through the swiping mechanisms on dating apps, can lead to considerable emotional distress. Users may internalize this rejection, associating it with their sense of value and diminishing their overall confidence. The anonymity of online interactions might encourage a culture where ghosting has become commonplace, exacerbating feelings of inadequacy and loneliness. These negative consequences underline the complexities of navigating emotions in a digital dating landscape, illustrating that the thrill of connection can rapidly transform into the pain of rejection. The continuous cycle of trying and failing to connect can instill a defensive attitude in individuals, leading to an increase in cynicism toward future romantic prospects. This emotional withdrawal, often a protective strategy, further complicates the quest for meaningful relationships. When users adopt a more guarded approach, they risk missing potential connections that could have been fulfilling. Studies indicate that individuals who experience repeated online rejection may become less willing to engage fully with future matches, viewing dating as a numbers game rather than an opportunity for genuine connection. This shift can manifest in a gap between desired outcomes and actual experiences, leaving many feeling unfulfilled. As users interact with the pervasive algorithms that prioritize match frequency over meaningful compatibility, they often find themselves caught in an endless loop of superficial encounters, where deeper emotional ties and authentic experiences remain elusive. Confronting the negative ramifications of rejection in online dating necessitates a reevaluation of personal expectations and coping strategies. Developing resilience in the face of emotional setbacks can help individuals navigate the highs and lows of dating in a more balanced manner. This mindset involves reframing rejection not as a reflection of personal worth, but rather as a natural part of the dating journey, allowing for growth and self-discovery. Engaging in self-reflection, seeking supportive social networks, and practicing self-care can help mitigate the adverse effects of rejection. Fostering an understanding that online dating is often fraught with misrepresentations and unrealistic expectations can enable users to approach potential matches with a healthier perspective. By embracing a more nuanced view of rejection and its implications, individuals can enhance their dating experiences, transforming setbacks into opportunities for personal growth and increased emotional resilience.

## Emotional Labor in Online Interactions

In the realm of online dating, the concept of emotional labor has taken on new dimensions, necessitating a deeper understanding of how users navigate their emotional landscapes. Emotional labor involves managing one's feelings to fulfill the expectations set by social contexts, and in the digital dating world, this often translates to how individuals present themselves in profiles and during interactions. Users frequently engage in the emotional labor of crafting their online personas to appear more appealing, altering language, tone, and facial expressions to fit an idealized image. Research indicates that this performative aspect can lead to emotional dissonance, where users feel a disparity between their authentic selves and the personas they project online. This heightened form of presentation can be both exhausting and alienating, as individuals must continuously monitor their interactions to adhere to the expectations of others, ultimately impacting their self-esteem and emotional well-being. The implications of emotional labor extend beyond the individual, influencing the dynamics of online relationships. Users often find themselves engaging in a balance of empathy and authenticity while conversing with potential matches, simultaneously striving to appear relatable and genuine. This tension frequently results in what social scientists term emotional overload, wherein people feel pressured to respond in an overly enthusiastic or agreeable manner to keep the momentum of conversation alive. This demand may lead to superficial connections rather than meaningful bonds, as the emphasis shifts from genuine interaction to a struggle for acceptance and validation. When users are not entirely forthcoming about their feelings or experiences, the risk of misunderstandings and misalignments increases, complicating the quest for authentic connection amidst the pressures of emotional labor. Navigating emotional labor within the context of online dating requires critical self-awareness and emotional intelligence. Users must recognize the fine line between presenting oneself positively and succumbing to the pressure of excessive performance. Reflection on one's motivations and feelings during online interactions can help mitigate the risks associated with emotional dissonance. Ensuring that ones online identity aligns closely with their true self can foster more authentic interactions and reduce the mental toll of managing expectations. Approaching online dating with an understanding of these dynamics may encourage individuals to engage in healthier communication patterns, focusing on genuine connections rather than mere surface-level compatibility. By valuing authenticity and emotional honesty, users can navigate the intricate landscape of online dating more effectively, ultimately enhancing the potential for finding meaningful, lasting relationships.

## Mental Health Considerations

Navigating the landscape of online dating can significantly

impact mental health, with both positive and negative implications for users. Those who find success in forging connections and enduring relationships often report boosts in self-esteem and overall happiness. The ability to interact with a diverse array of potential partners from the comfort of one's home can enhance feelings of empowerment, especially for individuals who may struggle to initiate conversations in traditional social settings. Online platforms provide a unique opportunity for self-expression and personal creativity, fostering a sense of belonging among individuals who might otherwise feel marginalized in their everyday environments. This potential for positive emotional growth can be undermined by the pressures and anxieties engendered by digital interactions, where rejection is often more palpable due to the rapidity of communication and the prevalence of ghosting, which can exacerbate feelings of inadequacy and loneliness. Conversely, reliance on online dating can lead to a series of mental health challenges that warrant critical examination. Many users are seduced by the illusion of endless options, yet this phenomenon can quickly morph into choice overload, causing anxiety and dissatisfaction. The constant comparison to polished profiles and carefully curated images contributes to feelings of inadequacy. The superficial nature of many interactions fosters a culture where individuals may focus more on quantity rather than quality of connections. This emphasis on physical attraction and compatibility often translates into a lack of depth in relationships, potentially leading to superficial bonds that leave individuals feeling unfulfilled. Such experiences can culminate in emotional exhaustion and a sense of disconnection, highlighting the importance of recognizing the psychological toll that online dating can impose while navigating its opportunities.

Understanding these psychological implications enriches the discourse surrounding online dating, particularly in terms of best practices for users to maintain their mental health. Acknowledging the pressures of social media narratives and the curated realities presented online is crucial for cultivating a realistic mindset about these platforms. Mindfulness strategies, such as limiting time spent on dating apps and focusing on genuine interactions, can help mitigate the negative effects of comparison and anxiety. Users should prioritize self-compassion, reminding themselves that rejection and mismatches are inevitable components of the dating process rather than reflections of personal worth. By adopting a balanced approach that emphasizes emotional well-being, individuals can navigate the complex dynamics of online dating more responsibly, ultimately enhancing their chances of fostering authentic and meaningful relationships. This awareness not only aids personal growth but also contributes to a healthier online dating culture that values genuine connections over superficial encounters.

# XIV. MYTH: YOU CAN FIND YOUR SOULMATE ONLINE

The allure of online dating platforms rests significantly on the notion of discovering ones soulmate with ease, but this myth oversimplifies the complexity of building genuine connections. Many users approach these platforms under the impression that a few well-crafted profile shots and witty bios are sufficient to encapsulate their true selves. In reality, these profiles often reduce individuals to a superficial collection of images and curated descriptions, which may not accurately reflect their personality, values, or compatibility. The algorithms designed to match users are based on basic preferences and popularity, often prioritizing physical attraction or desirability over deeper, more meaningful attributes. Consequently, this matching process frequently results in connections that lack substantive foundation, leading people to chase an elusive ideal of love rather than embarking on the more nuanced journey of understanding and connection that true romance requires. Further complicating this myth is the tendency for users to experience "choice overload" on these platforms. With countless options available, individuals may find themselves trapped in a paradox where the sheer volume of potential matches becomes overwhelming. This abundance can foster a fleeting psychological phenomenon known as the next best thing, where prospective partners are judged not for their intrinsic qualities or compatibility but rather as mere competitors in a match game, leading to a cycle of superficial engagement rather than sincere exploration. This constant search for an apparent soulmate can inhibit deeper emotional investments and the organic development of relationships. Users may swipe through profiles rapidly, driven by impulse, rather than taking the necessary time to engage with and appreciate potential partners personally, which can paradoxically lead to increased feelings of loneliness instead of fulfilling connections. The myth that one can effortlessly find a soulmate online disregards the importance of patience, communication, and vulnerability in the pursuit of meaningful relationships. True compatibility often flourishes in environments where individuals can gradually reveal their authentic selves and foster trust over time, aspects that are frequently lost in the fast-paced realm of online dating. For meaningful connections to develop, it is essential for users to approach these platforms with realistic expectations, recognizing that finding a soulmate is rarely a straightforward endeavor. Instead of focusing solely on algorithms or idealized profiles, it is crucial to embrace the process of dating itself—the ups and downs, the moments of discovery, and the gradual unfolding of affection. Understanding that real love requires effort, vulnerability, and time can shift the perspective on online dating from a quest for instant gratification to an opportunity for personal growth and a more profound emotional connection, ultimately paving the way for authentic relationships.

## Unrealistic Expectations of Online Dating

Navigating the world of online dating can often lead users to foster unattainable aspirations regarding romantic partnerships. The ease with which individuals can browse profiles and exchange messages may create an illusion that finding love is a matter of simply selecting suitable candidates. This perception can be misleading, as many people project an idealized version of themselves online, leading to a disconnect between reality and expectations. Statistics reveal that a significant proportion of individuals modify their profiles to emphasize appealing traits, thereby skewing the authenticity of initial interactions. Consequently, users may approach connections with an inflated sense of certainty, only to encounter the stark reality that many profiles are curated to portray an illusion rather than the genuine self. This misrepresentation often results in disappointment, reinforcing the notion that online platforms may not deliver compatible matches as effortlessly as expected. These inflated hopes regarding online dating are further exacerbated by the design of many dating platforms, which often prioritize instant gratification. The swipe culture, popularized by certain applications, encourages rapid decision-making based on superficial characteristics such as appearance. Users become conditioned to seek immediate feedback through matches or messages, which can erode their patience and alter their perception of what constitutes a suitable partner. This immediacy minimizes the importance of deeper connections and meaningful interactions, leading many to overlook potential relationships that may develop over time. When connections are primarily evaluated on fleeting judgments rather than compatibility or shared values, the likelihood of forming substantive relationships diminishes. The allure of quick matches may seduce users into dismissing individuals who could offer more enriching companionship. Detaching oneself from the unrealistic expectations perpetuated by online dating requires a critical reassessment of ones motivations and goals. A more mindful approach can foster healthier attitudes towards creating connections in the digital space.

Users should prioritize genuine interactions, focusing on individuals rather than superficial traits, while also being aware of the potential for curated façades. This shift in perspective can enable a more accurate understanding of online dating as a supplement to traditional relationship-building rather than a definitive solution for finding love. By grounding expectations in realistic terms—acknowledging that major connections take time and effort to cultivate—users can navigate online dating with a more balanced outlook. This conscious approach not only enhances the likelihood of discovering meaningful relationships but also helps mitigate the emotional pitfalls associated with disillusionment.

## The Concept of the "Perfect Match"

The allure of discovering a perfect match has become a central tenet of the online dating experience, capturing the imaginations of millions seeking love. This notion is largely perpetuated by dating platforms that promote compatibility through algorithms designed to identify shared interests and values among users. While this scientific approach can facilitate meaningful connections, it also raises questions about the depth of those relationships. Statistics show that users who place undue emphasis on algorithmic matches may overlook potential partners who, while lacking statistical compatibility, could foster a more profound emotional bond. Consequently, the concept of the perfect match risks oversimplifying human connection, reducing the complexities of relationships to data points rather than the intricate dance of human emotions and experiences. The expectation of finding an ideal partner often comes with unrealistic pressures, as many individuals turn to these platforms with preconceived notions about love and compatibility. The digital facade of profiles can amplify these expectations, as users curate their images and narratives, sometimes presenting an unrealistic version of themselves. This phenomenon not only misleads potential partners but also creates an environment of superficiality, where genuine human connection can be sacrificed in favor of first-impression aesthetics. Research indicates that the vast array of choices provided by online dating can lead to a paradox of choice, causing individuals to be less satisfied with their decisions, as they constantly search for a "better" option rather than investing in developing an existing connection. Thus, the quest for a perfect match may inadvertently foster a cycle of discontent and superficial interactions, undermining the foundations of lasting relationships. The evolving nature of interpersonal relationships in the digital landscape challenges the very essence of what it means to be a "perfect match." The expectations surrounding this title often prioritize immediate gratification over long-term compatibility. It is essential to recognize that successful relationships are built on shared experiences, effective communication, and mutual growth rather than solely on algorithmic compatibility or physical attraction. Emphasizing the importance of emotional intelligence, vulnerability, and patience can enhance the likelihood of forming meaningful connections in an online setting. As users navigate these platforms, a shift in focus from an idealized notion of romance to a more holistic understanding of partnership can lead to healthier and more sustainable relationships. The reality of finding love online lies not in the pursuit of perfection but in embracing the imperfections that make each connection unique and valuable.

# The Role of Compatibility in Relationships

A critical element that often shapes the success of romantic partnerships is the concept of compatibility. This multifaceted notion encompasses various dimensions, including emotional, intellectual, and lifestyle factors, which together serve to foster deeper connections between individuals. Emotional compatibility refers to the ability to understand and resonate with each others feelings, allowing partners to navigate conflicts and express affection effectively. Meanwhile, intellectual compatibility involves the alignment of values, beliefs, and interests, which can enhance conversation and shared experiences. Lifestyle compatibility can influence day-to-day interactions, as differing habits, priorities, or goals may lead to friction. Online dating platforms, while ostensibly designed to facilitate these connections, may not always provide the nuanced understanding required to gauge compatibility accurately, prompting users to question whether their matches are truly a good fit. Interactions on dating apps often prioritize immediate attraction and superficial traits, which can overshadow the deeper compatibility necessary for lasting relationships. Users are frequently enticed by visually appealing profiles and catchy bios, inadvertently leading them to favor short-term satisfaction over long-term connection. This phenomenon is exacerbated by algorithmic matchmaking that emphasizes surface-level similarities rather than deeper emotional and intellectual bonds. Consequently, many users may find themselves trapped in cycles of fleeting encounters that fail to develop into substantial relationships. Research indicates that while initial attraction is essential, partners who lack deeper compatibility often struggle with enduring issues later in their relationship. Thus, the emphasis on surface-level characteristics in online dating may contribute to a skewed perception of compatibility, leaving individuals disillusioned when efforts to establish meaningful connections fall short. Addressing the disparity between perceived and actual compatibility is crucial for enhancing relationship success in the digital dating landscape. Users must approach online platforms with a discernible focus on genuine connection rather than merely fulfilling a checklist of desirable traits. This entails engaging in self-reflection to understand one's own values and desires adequately while remaining open to exploring the nuances of prospective partners beyond their profiles. Fostering authentic connections may require patience and a willingness to engage in deeper conversations early in the interaction. By actively pursuing a more comprehensive understanding of compatibility, individuals can mitigate the superficial tendencies of digital dating, paving the way for more meaningful and lasting relationships. This awareness serves not only to improve personal experiences but also to counteract the myths surrounding love and connection in the modern dating arena.

# XV. TRUTH: ONLINE DATING REQUIRES EFFORT

In the realm of online dating, initial impressions are often misleading, which contributes to the notion that finding a meaningful relationship requires minimal effort. Many users are lured in by the allure of potentially effortless matchmaking, facilitated by algorithms designed to curate compatible partners. This convenience can result in superficial connections that lack depth. Engaging genuinely with potential matches mandates a commitment to foster deeper relationships, requiring time and emotional investment. Participants must actively participate in conversations, share meaningful experiences, and be open to vulnerability, rather than relying exclusively on surface-level interactions. The stark disparity between expectations and reality highlights that truly connecting with others online often necessitates the same level of diligence as traditional dating methods. Effective communication plays a pivotal role in the success of online dating endeavors. Crafting a profile that accurately reflects one's personality and intentions is the first critical step, yet the process does not cease there. Initiating conversations that move beyond banal pleasantries calls for creativity and attentiveness to the other persons interests or experiences. Developing rapport through thoughtful questions and responses demonstrates genuine investment in the relationship, which can bolster the chance of progressing to a deeper connection. Despite the seemingly infinite pool of potential matches, the absence of authentic engagement can lead to disconnect, leaving many individuals disillusioned with their online dating experiences. Hence, recognizing that meaningful interactions require deliberate effort is crucial for anyone navigating the complexities of digital romance. The culmination of these efforts ultimately informs how individuals perceive the landscape of modern dating. When users approach online platforms armed with the understanding that honest communication and emotional vulnerability are essential, they can significantly enhance their likelihood of finding lasting connections. Recognizing the necessity of a proactive stance can help dispel the myth that genuine love can be attained with minimal exertion. Instead, by approaching these platforms with realistic expectations and a preparedness to invest time and energy, individuals are more likely to cultivate authentic relationships that transcend initial encounters. This shift in perspective not only enriches the online dating experience but also fosters a healthier understanding of what it means to seek companionship in a digital world.

## The Importance of Active Engagement

Active engagement plays a crucial role in fostering meaningful connections, especially in the realm of online dating. Many users approach these platforms with unrealistic expectations, often looking for instant gratification rather than investing time and effort into building genuine relationships. Engaging actively with potential partners entails more than just swiping right or sending a few superficial messages. It involves open communication, vulnerability, and an authentic representation of oneself. Studies show that individuals who share personal stories and express genuine interest in their matches tend to form stronger bonds. This deeper level of interaction not only enhances the likelihood of compatibility but also creates an environment where both parties feel comfortable and valued, laying the foundation for a potential long-term relationship. The prevalence of algorithms in online dating underscores the necessity for intentional participation. While many platforms promise to streamline the matchmaking process based on user preferences and behaviors, they cannot replicate the nuanced understanding that comes from direct human interaction. Active engagement can help mitigate the detrimental effects of algorithmic biases, which may inadvertently prioritize superficial traits over substantial compatibility factors. Engaging in thoughtful conversations can enable users to assess common values and interests—elements that are often overlooked when profiles are based solely on curated images or brief bios. By making a conscious effort to delve deeper into conversations and explore shared experiences, users can ultimately override the limitations imposed by algorithm-driven suggestions and forge connections that align more authentically with their desires and expectations. The shift from passive consumption to active engagement in online dating can reshape the overall landscape of romantic relationships formed through these platforms. In an age where superficial judgments abound, the ability to actively participate in ones dating life promotes emotional intelligence and self-awareness. Recognizing that dating requires a proactive approach allows individuals to redefine their romantic goals and set clearer expectations—all of which are essential in navigating the complexities of such interactions. When users invest time and effort into cultivating connections, they are more likely to attract matches receptive to deeper engagement as well. In essence, embracing active engagement not only enhances personal dating experiences but can also contribute to fostering a culture that values authenticity and meaningful connections amidst the rapid, often fleeting nature of online relationships.

## Strategies for Successful Online Dating

Success in online dating heavily relies on a strategic approach to profile creation. An engaging, authentic profile acts as the foundation for attracting potential matches. Users should invest time in crafting a balanced narrative that highlights their interests, values, and personality traits while remaining honest and inviting. High-quality photographs are crucial; a variety of images showcasing different aspects of life—such as hobbies, travel, or social settings—can provide a more holistic view of oneself. Individuals should avoid overly filtered or misleading images that might give a false impression. The choice of language in the profile description can shape a user's perceived compatibility, so incorporating humor or warmth can foster a connection. The goal is to balance openness and authenticity, allowing potential partners to see the genuine personality behind the profile, setting the stage for meaningful interactions. Effective communication plays a paramount role in online dating success and should be approached with intention. Initiating conversation based on shared interests or specific details mentioned in a profile often helps to break the ice and encourages more thorough dialogue. Thoughtful questions invite deeper exchanges, moving beyond superficial banter to explore values, aspirations, and personal experiences. It is essential to maintain a consistent tone that reflects one's true self while remaining respectful and considerate. Active listening during conversations ensures that both parties feel valued and understood, creating an atmosphere conducive to building rapport. Miscommunication can lead to misunderstandings, so being mindful of language and tone is critical. Its beneficial to recognize the importance of navigating the balance between enthusiasm and caution, as revealing too much too soon can overwhelm or alienate potential matches, while being too reserved may inhibit connection. Understanding the timing and pacing of interactions is crucial for sustaining interest in online dating. After establishing initial connections, individuals should avoid the temptation to rush into meeting in person without sufficient groundwork. This caution allows both parties to assess compatibility through ongoing dialogue and mutual discovery. When the decision is made to meet face-to-face, choosing a safe, casual, and public setting can alleviate anxiety while facilitating organic interaction. Remaining open-minded during these early encounters is vital; potential matches may not initially meet all preconceived expectations. Instead of adhering rigidly to idealized notions of romance, allowing space for unexpected chemistry or connection can lead to fruitful relationships. Practicing patience and maintaining a realistic outlook on dating timelines can also mitigate the pressures that often accompany seeking love online, paving the way for a more fulfilling and authentic dating experience that transcends the digital realm.

## Balancing Online and Offline Efforts

The interplay between online and offline efforts in the pursuit of romance is crucial in navigating the complexities of modern dating. Online platforms provide a vast array of opportunities for connection, allowing users to meet people outside their immediate social circles. This digital engagement can create a paradox wherein individuals may become overly reliant on virtual interactions, neglecting the vital nuances of face-to-face communication. Building authentic relationships often hinges on in-person experiences, where non-verbal cues, emotional resonance, and shared activities can occur. Striking a balance between engaging with online tools for initial connections and investing time in real-world interactions is imperative for cultivating meaningful relationships that go beyond superficial engagements. Empirical research highlights that while online dating can broaden one's dating pool, it can also lead to decision fatigue and superficial judgments. With countless profiles available at a swipe, users often find themselves comparing potential partners based solely on curated images and vague bios. This can foster a culture of disposability, where individuals are quick to discard prospective matches due to minor discrepancies, rather than pursuing deeper connections. Insights from social psychology suggest that successful matchmaking involves not just algorithm-driven compatibility assessments, but also the capacity to engage in sustained interactions. Individuals should employ online platforms strategically, using them as a springboard for offline encounters, while being conscious of the limitations of the digital realm in forming lasting bonds. Engaging in offline activities can significantly enhance the quality of relationships developed through online platforms. Participating in shared interests—such as joining clubs, attending social events, or volunteering—provides natural settings for meaningful connections to unfold. These environments encourage authenticity, allowing individuals to showcase their true selves beyond the polished versions often presented online. In-person interactions can significantly enrich the emotional depth of connections, fostering trust, empathy, and understanding. Moving beyond the mere act of texting or exchanging messages, the tactile experience of shared adventures and conversations can solidify relationships that began in the digital landscape. Integrating online efforts with offline activities promotes a holistic approach to dating, encouraging individuals to cultivate genuine relationships rooted in shared experiences and mutual understanding.

# XVI. MYTH: ONLINE DATING IS ONLY FOR HOOKUPS

A common assumption about online dating is that its primary purpose is to facilitate casual encounters rather than meaningful relationships. This perspective often overlooks the diverse motivations that individuals bring to these platforms. For many users, online dating serves as a convenient avenue to meet potential partners who share similar interests and values, whether they are seeking long-term commitment or companionship. Studies have shown that a significant segment of online daters report intentions of finding serious relationships, contradicting the stereotype that these platforms are merely hookup apps. In fact, many dating sites have tailored their algorithms to foster deeper connections by enabling users to filter potential matches based on relationship goals and compatibility factors, thereby shaping a more intentional dating experience. While stereotypes persist, the reality is that many people engaged in online dating possess an earnest desire for stable relationships. This demographic includes individuals who may find traditional dating avenues unsatisfactory due to busy lifestyles or geographical limitations. Online platforms grant users access to broader social networks, facilitating the discovery of like-minded individuals who might not have crossed paths otherwise. Communication tools available through these platforms allow for gradual acquaintance, which can lead to more substantial emotional and intellectual connections. Many users report that the time spent exchanging messages and getting to know each other builds a stronger foundation for a romantic relationship, challenging the narrative that online dating is solely about superficial encounters. The accountability of user profiles and community standards on reputable dating sites further challenges the myth of online dating as solely a hookup culture. Many platforms employ verification measures and prompts that encourage users to portray themselves authentically, creating an environment that fosters trustworthiness and respect. By emphasizing shared values and meaningful interactions, these platforms can facilitate connections that evolve into lasting partnerships. In fact, recent studies indicate that couples who meet online often report higher satisfaction levels and greater commitment compared to those who meet through traditional avenues. This illustrates that online dating can indeed yield profound and lasting love, debunking the prevailing myth and showcasing its potential for cultivating genuine relationships.

## Misconceptions About Intentions

Amid the myriad of expectations that accompany online dating, one prevalent misconception is that participants inherently possess the same intentions. Often, users assume that everyone on a dating platform is seeking a committed relationship, leading to misunderstandings when motivations diverge. While one person may be earnest in their search for love, another might simply be looking for casual companionship or validation. This disparity can result in confusion and disappointment, as relationships formed under different understandings of intent can crumble under the weight of unmet expectations. The anonymity of online interactions can exacerbate the situation, as individuals may feel emboldened to present themselves in ways that do not align with their true intentions. Disentangling these varied motivations requires open communication and honest dialogue, reminding users that their assumptions about others desires may not reflect reality. Another commonly held belief is that digital platforms foster meaningful connections more effectively than traditional dating methods. Users often envision that algorithms curate potential matches based on deep-seated compatibility, thereby enhancing their chances of finding a significant partner. The reality is frequently less romantic. Many algorithms prioritize superficial attributes, such as appearance or location, diminishing the focus on emotional or intellectual compatibility. Consequently, while users might experience a larger quantity of matches, this does not guarantee quality or depth in their interactions. The illusion of having countless options can lead to an overwhelming choice paralysis, where the abundance of potential partners overshadows the significance of forging a genuine connection. Thus, while online dating can extend ones social network and introduce novel encounters, it often does so at the risk of fostering connections that lack substantial grounding. The myth that online dating is a quick fix for loneliness or a guaranteed path to love can create unrealistic expectations that obscure the complexities of developing authentic relationships. Users often enter these environments with the hope of swiftly meeting a compatible partner, yet this impulsive approach can undermine the foundational elements necessary for lasting intimacy. Building a genuine connection typically requires time, effort, and vulnerability, qualities that can become diminished in the swipe-driven culture of online dating. The absence of face-to-face interactions can lead to misconceptions about compatibility, as users may project idealized versions of themselves while failing to engage in crucial self-reflection. As such, it is vital for individuals engaging in the digital dating landscape to

119

embrace a more nuanced understanding of relationships, recognizing the merits of patience and gradually unfolding connections rather than seeking instant gratification, which rarely yields fulfilling outcomes.

## The Spectrum of Relationship Goals

Navigating the complexities of contemporary relationships necessitates an understanding of diverse relationship goals that individuals possess. Many people approach dating with distinct objectives that can vary widely, from seeking long-term commitments to casual encounters. Recognizing these varied aspirations is crucial in dissecting the dynamics of online dating. Some users might join dating apps with the sole intention of exploring their options and enjoying the freedom of non-committed interactions, while others actively seek enduring partnerships. This spectrum not only illustrates the variety of desires but also emphasizes the potential for misunderstanding when two individuals are not aligned in their goals. Consequently, the online dating realm is marked by a multitude of expectations and intentions, making it imperative for individuals to articulate their desires clearly to foster meaningful connections. The appeal of convenience offered by online dating platforms often transmutes the essence of personal connections into transactional interactions. Users frequently find themselves interacting with a series of profiles that present curated versions of individuals, often rich in superficial attributes. This way, the focus may shift toward immediate gratification rather than fostering genuine emotional bonds. As the algorithms behind these platforms streamline this process, they inadvertently contribute to a culture that prizes speed over depth, particularly when users are inundated with choices. Such an environment can lead individuals to feel overwhelmed, resulting in a paradox where the abundance of options diminishes the perceived value of a unique, authentic relationship. Thus, the digital dating landscape can inadvertently promote a superficial understanding of love, complicating the journey toward genuine fulfillment and satisfaction in relational pursuits. The misalignment between users intentions and their perceptions can culminate in disillusionment and frustration. In attempts to navigate the vast landscape of online romance, many individuals may find themselves disheartened by the disparity between their expectations and the reality of their experiences. Misrepresentation in profiles, stemming from the pressure to appear more appealing, can lead to trust issues and a skewed understanding of romance. The phenomenon of ghosting, where one party abruptly ends communication, intensifies feelings of uncertainty and insecurity among users. Such experiences highlight the importance of cultivating resilience and realistic expectations in the digital dating sphere. Encouraging users to engage in self-reflection about their relationship goals fosters healthier interactions. Embracing a more grounded approach towards online dating can significantly enrich one's journey to find meaningful love, amidst the challenges posed by the current digital landscape.

# Research on Relationship Outcomes

Examining the dynamics of relationship outcomes in the context of online dating reveals a fascinating interplay between technology and interpersonal connections. A critical component of this investigation lies in understanding how varying communication patterns impact relationship satisfaction and longevity.

Research indicates that couples who engage in richer, more diverse forms of communication—whether through phone calls, video chats, or face-to-face meetings—report higher levels of relationship satisfaction compared to those who rely solely on text-based interactions. The anonymity and perceived distance of online platforms can hinder deeper emotional bonds, fostering a reliance on surface-level interactions that may prove inadequate for meaningful connections. Consequently, the outcomes of these digitally cultivated relationships often correlate with the communication modalities chosen by the individuals, underscoring the importance of balancing digital interaction with authentic, in-person engagement. The influence of algorithms on relationship outcomes cannot be overlooked, as these systems significantly shape user experiences on dating platforms. Algorithms are designed to curate potential matches based on users profiles and preferences, ostensibly aiming to optimize compatibility. Studies suggest that this mechanization can inadvertently perpetuate a cycle of superficiality, leading users to prioritize aesthetic appeal and initial attraction over deeper personality traits. This emphasis on algorithm-driven choices may create a false sense of efficiency in the dating process, breeding unrealistic expectations of swift connection and instant gratification. The reliance on algorithms could undermine the inherent complexities of human relationships, affecting the stability and depth of the bonds that emerge from these initial matches. Understanding the nuances of algorithmic influence is therefore essential in evaluating how these technology-mediated interactions affect the overall quality and sustainability of relationships. In studying the narratives of individuals navigating online dating, a common theme of myth and reality emerges that shapes their expectations and experiences. Many users enter the digital dating landscape with preconceived notions about finding the one quickly and effortlessly. Qualitative research reveals a more nuanced reality, with many individuals encountering challenges such as misrepresentation, emotional detachment, or a lack of chemistry despite initial matches. By confronting these disparities between expectation and reality, users can develop a more informed approach to online dating. This shift not only encourages realistic assessments of potential partners but also helps to foster resilience in the face of disappointments commonly associated with the pursuit of love in a digital space. Thus, integrating these insights into ones dating strategy may lead to healthier relationship outcomes, empowering individuals to approach online connections with both optimism and pragmatism.

# XVII. TRUTH: CULTURAL DIFFERENCES IN ONLINE DATING

When delving into the dynamics of online dating, it is essential to recognize that perceptions of truth vary significantly across cultures. In many Western nations, users often emphasize authenticity and self-disclosure, presenting a curated, yet relatively genuine representation of themselves. This culture prioritizes individualism, leading to a tendency for profiles that highlight personal achievements and aspirations as a way to attract potential partners. In contrast, some Eastern cultures may prioritize familial expectations and social conformity, resulting in online dating profiles that reflect broader community values rather than purely individual traits. This divergence can lead to misunderstandings when individuals from differing cultural backgrounds engage on the same platform, potentially complicating the dating experience. The inherent biases in algorithms used by these dating apps can exacerbate these cultural differences by perpetuating stereotypes and limiting users to a narrow range of profiles that may not align with their deeper values or expectations. The concept of honesty in online dating is also deeply influenced by cultural narratives surrounding romance and relationships. In cultures where romantic relationships are heavily influenced by tradition and societal norms, presenting a truthful portrayal can be more complex. In some collectivist societies, individuals might feel pressured to present themselves in ways that align with communal standards, often sacrificing personal truths in the process. On the other hand, in cultures that valorize independence and open-mindedness, users might be more inclined to experiment with their identities, presenting exaggerated or even fictitious aspects of themselves in an effort to stand out. This juxtaposition leads to a frequently turbulent dating landscape, where users on international platforms confront conflicting expectations that may shape their online interactions. Consequently, the search for truth in this context becomes a multi-faceted challenge, requiring keen awareness of cultural implications that inform personal presentation and relational dynamics. Navigating these contrasting cultural norms is crucial for anyone seeking love in the digital age. To enhance the likelihood of meaningful connections, users must cultivate cultural sensitivity and awareness, recognizing the diverse backgrounds and experiences of potential matches. Engaging in open dialogue about expectations, values, and intentions not only fosters transparency but can also lead to deeper conversations that break down barriers of misunderstanding. It is also beneficial to approach online dating with a critical lens, being mindful of how personal biases may distort perceptions of truth. Educating oneself about cultural differences in dating practices can empower individuals to approach online platforms with greater empathy and realism, reducing the likelihood of disillusionment. A proactive approach that prioritizes understanding and communication can transform the online dating landscape into a more authentic and fulfilling experience, where love can be discovered amidst the complexities of cultural differences.

## Variations in Dating Norms Across Cultures

Cultural interpretations of romance and courtship significantly shape individuals dating experiences globally. In some societies, dating serves as a platform for maintaining familial connections and community expectations. Many cultures emphasize arranged marriages, wherein families play a crucial role in selecting partners. Within this framework, dating occurs with the intention of assessing compatibility and meeting parental approval rather than individual desire. Conversely, western cultures often promote the concept of dating as a personal journey rooted in individual choice and romantic exploration. In these contexts, dating functions as a preliminary stage before a serious commitment, allowing for self-discovery and emotional intimacy. The stark contrast in dating practices illuminates how cultural backgrounds can influence expectations and behaviors, with implications for those using online dating platforms. Understanding these differences is essential not only for fostering healthy relationships but also for navigating potential cultural misunderstandings in the pursuit of love. The communication styles within different cultures further complicate the dynamics of dating. In many Asian cultures, indirect communication is preferred, and expressions of affection may be subtle, prioritizing modesty and reserve. Here, dating often incorporates cultural rituals and traditions, with an emphasis on building trust and rapport over time, contrasting sharply with more direct and assertive approaches seen in many Western cultures. The latter often celebrate overt expressions of interest through casual dating scenarios, where flirtation and open communication are the norms. This disparity can lead to misinterpretations when individuals engage in online dating, as varying expectations can result in confusion about intentions. As users navigate the digital dating landscape, recognizing these nuances becomes essential for ensuring respectful interactions and mutual understanding. It further underscores the need for increased cultural competency among those seeking meaningful connections in the evolving landscape of modern romance. The rise of digital platforms has introduced a new layer of complexity to the cultural variations in dating norms. Online dating applications allow users to transcend geographical boundaries, connecting individuals from vastly different cultural backgrounds. This interconnectedness can both enrich the dating experience through exposure to diverse perspectives and challenge participants to reconcile differing expectations regarding courtship and relationship development. As individuals encounter others from cultures with distinct protocols for dating, they may inadvertently face pressure to conform to unfamiliar customs. Spontaneous date invitations typical in some western cultures might be perceived as disrespectful or too forward in more conservative societies. The potential for misunderstanding highlights the necessity for informed discourse around cultural norms within the online dating sphere. As users become more aware of these variances, they can engage in more thoughtful interactions, fostering connections built on appreciation and authentic understanding rather than cultural ignorance.

## The Influence of Cultural Backgrounds

In the multifaceted landscape of online dating, cultural backgrounds play a significant role in shaping user experiences and expectations. These influences are deeply embedded within individual identities and are often reflected in dating preferences, communication styles, and even the types of relationships sought. Individuals from collectivist cultures may prioritize family approval and communal aspects in their dating lives, seeking partners who align with those values. Conversely, those from more individualistic societies may focus on personal fulfillment and autonomy. This divergence not only affects how people present themselves on dating platforms but also impacts the ways in which they interpret potential matches. Understanding these differences is crucial, as the algorithms used by dating apps often fail to account for the nuances of cultural expectations, risking miscommunication and discouragement among users who might not find matches that resonate with their backgrounds. Expectations stemming from cultural backgrounds can also manifest in the choice of language and expressions employed in online interactions. For many users, the way they communicate reveals significant cultural markers—such as humor, formality, or directness—that influence their dating experiences. A person raised in a culture that values straightforward communication may find themselves frustrated by the more subtle, suggestive styles common in other contexts. This disparity can lead to misunderstandings and misinterpretations, potentially derailing promising connections before they have a chance to blossom. The pressure to conform to one's cultural norms while navigating the paradox of being anonymous on dating sites can complicate the authenticity of user interactions. As such, the blending of cultural expectations with the fast-paced nature of digital interactions necessitates a more nuanced understanding of online dating that considers the cultural underpinnings that shape individual behaviors. Acknowledging the intricate interplay of cultural backgrounds within the realm of online dating enhances the understanding of its complexities. As users engage with these platforms, they bring with them a tapestry of beliefs, customs, and values that influence their romantic pursuits. This cultural contextualization not only enriches the discussion around online dating but also highlights the importance of broader social adaptability in these digital spaces. Awareness of ones own cultural biases—as well as those of potential partners—can serve as a foundation for fostering deeper connections that transcend superficial attributes often emphasized in online profiles. By prioritizing cultural sensitivity and open communication, users can navigate the online dating landscape more effectively, cultivating relationships that honor their diverse backgrounds while bridging the gaps that technology may create.

## Cross-Cultural Dating Experiences

Navigating the intricate landscape of cross-cultural dating can prove both exhilarating and challenging. The melding of diverse cultural backgrounds often enriches a relationship, introducing partners to new traditions, values, and perspectives. These differences can also lead to misunderstandings. While some cultures prioritize family approval in relationships, others may emphasize individual choice. This clash of priorities may create tension, especially when one partner perceives the other's family-centric behaviors as excessive or intrusive. Successful navigation of these cultural nuances often hinges on effective communication. Empathy and a willingness to learn about each other's traditions and values can strengthen the bond formed through online platforms. While the dynamics of cross-cultural dating may at times seem daunting, embracing these challenges can lead to a deeper understanding and appreciation of one another. Many individuals approach online dating with preconceived notions shaped by societal influences and personal experiences. These myths can distort expectations, particularly in cross-cultural contexts. One prevalent myth is that cultural differences will inherently lead to conflict, limiting the prospects for lasting love. In reality, many couples flourish due to their ability to negotiate and harmonize their varying cultural beliefs. By uncovering shared values and celebrating differences, partners can create a unique dynamic that fosters mutual respect and admiration. Research supports this notion; studies have shown that couples who navigate cultural differences often experience heightened levels of emotional intelligence and adaptability. By dismantling these myths, individuals can foster realistic expectations and embark on their dating journeys with a more open mindset, increasing the likelihood of successful, fulfilling relationships across cultures. The role of technology and digital platforms in cross-cultural dating has become increasingly significant in today's globalized world. Online dating apps have not only expanded access to a diverse pool of potential partners but also facilitated the breaking down of geographical barriers. The freedom to interact with individuals from different backgrounds encourages inclusivity and connection. It also necessitates that users confront issues of representation and authenticity. Profiles may not always convey the entirety of a persons identity and cultural background, leading to potential misinterpretations. Thus, it becomes vital for individuals to approach online interactions with a willingness to engage beyond the surface. By fostering genuine curiosity and openness, daters can bridge cultural gaps and cultivate meaningful relationships. While technology has enhanced the diversity of romantic possibilities, it necessitates a critical approach to ensure authenticity and sincere connection.

# XVIII. MYTH: ALL DATING APPS ARE THE SAME

Many individuals often enter the realm of online dating with a generalized perception that all dating apps serve the same purpose because they primarily aim to connect individuals seeking romantic relationships. This perspective disregards the significant differences in how these platforms function, their target populations, and the specific features they offer. While apps like Tinder prioritize casual encounters and quick matches based on geographical proximity, platforms such as eHarmony and Match cater to users looking for long-term relationships, emphasizing compatibility through elaborate questionnaires. The categorization of these apps is not merely superficial; it reflects deeper underlying philosophies in their designs that play a crucial role in shaping user experiences and expectations. Thus, conflating all dating apps into one homogeneous category limits users understanding of the diverse dating landscape, which can result in misplaced expectations and ultimately unsuccessful encounters. In reality, the mechanisms that drive user engagement on these platforms vary significantly, affecting how relationships are formed and sustained. Certain apps employ complex algorithms that suggest potential matches based on behavior patterns and preferences, while others may rely more heavily on user-generated criteria, allowing for greater agency in choice. Hinge, an app branded as designed to be deleted, encourages meaningful connections through prompts that facilitate deeper conversations, which inherently contrasts with a platform like Bumble, where women initiate the conversation after a match, thereby empowering users with differing dynamics. These distinctions are crucial, as they not only influence the type of interactions users encounter but also reflect broader societal attitudes toward dating and relationships. Misunderstanding these varied approaches can lead one to presume that digital interactions will yield the same depth or satisfaction, when in reality, they vary widely based on the apps unique framework and guiding philosophy. Recognizing that dating apps are not uniformly effective for all users illuminates critical insights regarding individual dating goals and relationship dynamics in the digital age. Some platforms cater specifically to niche communities, such as LGBTQ+ individuals, vegetarians, or those seeking faith-based partnerships. By delivering tailored experiences, these apps foster environments where users feel more comfortable expressing their identities and navigating relationships. If users approach these platforms with a mindset that equates them all, they may overlook opportunities specifically aligned with their interests, potentially fostering disappointment or frustration. As the landscape of online dating continues to evolve, misunderstandings about the nature and purpose of various apps can hinder individuals from engaging with technological advancements designed to improve their experiences. By debunking this myth, users can make informed decisions that not only enhance their dating journeys but also contribute to a richer understanding of how love can manifest in our increasingly digital societal context.

## Differences Between Dating Platforms

The landscape of online dating is diverse, with platforms catering to various demographics and relationship goals. Each dating site or app has unique characteristics that influence user experience and engagement. Services like Tinder and Bumble primarily appeal to younger users seeking casual relationships or quick interactions. These platforms utilize swiping mechanisms, emphasizing physical attraction and immediacy. In contrast, apps like eHarmony and Match.com focus on longer-term commitments, employing comprehensive questionnaires to gauge compatibility based on values, beliefs, and interests. This difference in approach underscores a fundamental divergence in target audiences: while some platforms prioritize speed and superficiality, others advocate for deep, meaningful connections. Users must navigate this array of options to select a platform that aligns not only with their relationship intentions but also with their individual personalities and lifestyles. Notably, the algorithms driving these platforms also dramatically shape the dating experience. Algorithms on platforms like OkCupid and Hinge utilize complex data analytics to match users based on compatibility scores derived from extensive user input. This data-driven approach highlights the growing importance of technology in romantic endeavors, as it aims to filter potential partners more efficiently than traditional means. While these algorithms can enhance prospective matches, they are not infallible. Users may find themselves overwhelmed by the sheer volume of potential partners presented to them, diluting the quality of interactions. The reliance on algorithms raises concerns about the superficiality of connections, as users may prioritize algorithm-generated matches over authentic compatibility. Thus, understanding these technological frameworks is essential for navigating the nuances of modern dating effectively. The social implications of varying dating platforms cannot be overlooked. Platforms tailored for specific niches, such as Grindr for the

LGBTQ+ community or FarmersOnly for rural singles, create spaces where users can engage in authentic connections that might be harder to forge in broader contexts. These niche platforms also reproduce certain social dynamics, including exclusivity and bias. Users might find themselves confined to a limited pool of potential partners who share similar backgrounds or lifestyles, which can lead to a lack of diversity and experience. The culture instilled by these platforms—ranging from a focus on aesthetics to the stigma around online dating—can affect self-esteem and approach to relationships. As individuals engage in this digital dating landscape, it is crucial to remain mindful of both the empowering and limiting aspects that different platforms present in the pursuit of lasting love.

## Target Audiences of Various Apps

In the realm of mobile applications designed for romance, a distinct categorization of target audiences emerges, each reflecting a varying set of needs and aspirations. Platforms like Tinder and Bumble often cater to younger populations, particularly those in their late teens and twenties. These users are typically seeking casual encounters or relationships that can manifest quickly and with relative ease. The immediacy of swipe-based interactions resonates with a generation accustomed to fast-paced digital communication. By contrast, apps such as eHarmony or Match.com appeal to older demographics, often in their thirties and forties, who prioritize long-term commitment and emotional compatibility. This divergence in target audiences influences the marketing strategies these platforms employ, with casual apps emphasizing fun and spontaneity, while more serious platforms highlight features like compatibility algorithms and extensive questionnaires. The user experience within each app is meticulously tailored to its intended demographic, further solidifying its brand identity in a crowded market. Casual dating applications often streamline the interface, focusing on visually driven profiles that encourage quick engagement. The emphasis on profiles dominated by images caters to users looking for immediate attraction rather than in-depth compatibility analysis. In contrast, platforms aimed at serious relationships tend to incorporate comprehensive personality assessments and detailed questionnaires. This approach serves to foster an environment of thoughtful connection, appealing to users who are willing to invest time in understanding their potential partners. These structural differences reflect inherent expectations within each user group, making it clear that while dating apps seem homogenized, they operate on finely tuned principles that cater to the diverse romantic inclinations of their users. The perception of online dating and its corresponding platforms varies significantly across different age groups and cultural backgrounds. Younger individuals often express a sense of familiarity and ease with navigating these digital landscapes, viewing them as extensions of their social lives. Meanwhile, older users may experience skepticism regarding the authenticity of relationships formed online, primarily due to personal experiences or the societal stigma that has historically surrounded online dating. This duality in perception not only influences user engagement but also informs the narratives surrounding online relationships. As each demographic grapples with the realities of virtual romance, cultural factors become increasingly indispensable in shaping expectations and outcomes. In essence, understanding the diverse target audiences of various dating apps is crucial, as it directly impacts user experience, perception, and ultimately the success of finding meaningful connections in this vast digital landscape.

## Unique Features of Popular Apps

Understanding the distinctive features of popular dating apps reveals much about their broader implications for modern relationships. Often, these platforms employ sophisticated algorithms designed to analyze user data and preferences, which can significantly enhance the efficiency of matching potential partners. Apps like Tinder and Bumble utilize geolocation technology, allowing users to connect with others in their vicinity. This feature not only fosters spontaneous interactions but also cultivates a sense of immediacy, aligning with the fast-paced nature of contemporary society. This convenience can lead to a superficial culture where users prioritize quantity over quality in their romantic pursuits. As a result, while these algorithms promise a streamlined approach to finding love, they can inadvertently contribute to a transactional mindset that undermines deeper connections. Another defining characteristic of these platforms is their emphasis on visual content, often shaping user perceptions based on profile photos and brief bios. With apps like Hinge, the focus is on cultivating connections through more engaging profiles that encourage users to share snippets of their personalities, passions, and values. This characteristic aims to promote authentic interactions by moving beyond mere cursory evaluations based on appearances. Nevertheless, the reliance on images can foster an environment where superficial judgments prevail, often overshadowing the complexity of individuals behind the screens. Contrasting the curated nature of these profiles with the potential for misrepresentation raises concerns about authenticity in online dating. Users may inadvertently mislead others through deceptive photos or exaggerated descriptions, complicating the quest for genuine romantic connections. Popular dating apps incorporate social features that enhance the user experience by transforming the dating landscape into a more communal space. Platforms like Coffee Meets Bagel allow users to connect with common friends or acquaintances, effectively leveraging existing social networks to establish trust. This incorporation of social proof can make the dating process feel less daunting and more in line with traditional matchmaking methods. It also blurs the lines between casual dating and serious relationships, as users may feel pressured to conform to social expectations. While these apps can create a sense of belonging among users, they also risk amplifying insecurities about romance and relationships. The unique features of dating apps reflect both innovative conveniences and challenges that can shape users perceptions of love in this digital age, stressing the importance of utilizing these tools thoughtfully.

# XIX. TRUTH: THE ROLE OF SOCIAL MEDIA IN DATING

The proliferation of social media platforms has fundamentally reshaped how individuals perceive and engage in dating. With countless apps and websites at their fingertips, users are drawn into a realm where the notion of love is often corrupted by superficial interactions. Social media allows for a constant stream of images and status updates, creating a paradox of connection and loneliness. For many, the allure of instant gratification through likes and comments can diminish the value of deep, meaningful relationships. The curated profiles often present an idealized version of oneself, making it challenging to discern authenticity. Consequently, this emphasis on surface-level attraction can lead to disillusionment when expectations inevitably clash with reality, thus affecting users ability to form genuinely fulfilling connections. The algorithms utilized by dating platforms play a crucial role in shaping user experiences, often perpetuating a cyclical pattern of superficiality. These algorithms are designed to highlight profiles that align with users' preferences, which might reinforce a narrow standard of attractiveness and compatibility. While this approach can streamline the search process, it also limits exposure to diverse perspectives and experiences, thereby homogenizing potential matches. Users may find themselves entangled in an endless cycle of swiping, where quantity takes precedence over quality, ultimately hindering their ability to establish a strong emotional bond. This commodification of relationships can foster a transactional mindset; instead of seeking true companionship, individuals may instead chase an ever-elusive ideal, further distorting their

138

understanding of what a successful relationship involves. Despite these challenges, it is essential for users to cultivate an awareness of their digital interactions, leveraging social media for more meaningful connections. Awareness can be enhanced through self-reflection and mindfulness about one's expectations and motivations when engaging with online dating platforms. By approaching dating with a balance of optimism and caution, individuals can sift through the noise of superficial interactions and focus on establishing genuine connections that transcend the facade of digital personas. Engaging in conversations that delve deeper than surface appearances and seeking opportunities for in-person meetings can also mitigate the risks associated with online dating. A conscious and realistic approach to social media can help transform these platforms from mere sources of distraction into valuable tools for finding love and companionship that align with users true desires.

## Integration of Social Media and Dating

The seamless integration of social media into the realm of dating has significantly influenced how individuals initiate and cultivate romantic connections. Platforms like Instagram, Facebook, and Twitter do not merely serve as tools for communication; they have become essential facets of the online dating landscape. This convergence enables users to gather a more comprehensive picture of potential partners, often extending beyond the information provided in traditional dating profiles. Viewing someones posts, interests, and social interactions can reveal values, lifestyle choices, and personality traits that may not be articulated on a dating app. Consequently, potential matches can engage in deeper conversations based on observed commonalities, fostering a sense of connection before even meeting in person. This access to more context can also lead to the challenge of over-analyzing perceived red flags or misinterpreting social cues, complicating the dating process further and potentially leading to misunderstandings. While social media can enhance romantic interactions, it also engenders a culture of constant comparison and superficiality, which may distort perceptions of what constitutes a desirable partner. The visual nature of platforms often promotes an emphasis on physical appearance, leading users to judge potential matches based on curated images rather than genuine compatibility. This superficial engagement is further fueled by the addictive nature of scrolling through endless content, which creates a sense of choice overload. Research indicates that when individuals feel they have numerous options, they may struggle to commit to one partner, continually questioning whether a better match is just a click away. The portrayal of relationships on social media often presents an unrealistic ideal, pushing users to chase after infatuation rather than fostering authentic connections. This tendency can lead to dissatisfaction and disillusionment as users navigate their own dating experiences, revealing a significant drawback to integrating social media into romantic pursuits. The blurred lines between friendship and romantic interests complicate the dynamics of online dating, as social media fosters a dualistic environment where both relationships can coexist seamlessly. The ability to engage with friends and potential partners simultaneously allows users to develop connections that might naturally evolve into romance. This also creates pressure to manage expectations appropriately. Misinterpretations of platonic gestures as romantic advancements can lead to discomfort or anxiety in social settings. The public nature of social media interactions means that relationship statuses and dating journeys often become the subject of observation and speculation, adding an additional layer of complexity. Individuals may find themselves in situations where external validation, driven by likes or comments on their relationship posts, influences their perceived happiness. This illustrates the need for a mindful approach to dating in the digital age, underscoring the importance of balancing the social and personal aspects of finding love in a world increasingly dominated by online interactions.

## Impact of Social Media on Relationship Dynamics

Today's digital landscape is teeming with platforms that significantly shape personal interactions, particularly in romantic contexts. The prevalence of social media has transformed how individuals communicate and establish connections, often creating a paradox of increased connectivity alongside heightened emotional distance. Through instant messaging, likes, and shares, users curate their lives in a way that prioritizes visual representation over genuine connection. This shift can lead to the development of highly curated identities, where the realities of individuals are obscured, leading to skewed perceptions and potential misunderstandings. Research has shown that the brevity of interactions facilitated by social media can diminish the depth of communication, leading to surface-level exchanges instead of meaningful conversations. Consequently, the reliance on such mediums can warp relationship dynamics, as evidenced by increasing reports of misunderstandings and conflict stemming from misinterpretations of online communication. The addictive nature of social media often exacerbates insecurity within relationships, fueling a cycle of comparison and dissatisfaction. Couples frequently find themselves navigating the challenges posed by an overload of information and the pressure to present an idealized version of their romantic lives online. This constant scrutiny can breed jealousy and create unrealistic expectations, as individuals measure their relationships against the highly curated lives of others showcased on social platforms. The phenomenon of 'social comparison theory' illustrates how exposure to the seemingly perfect relationships of others can undermine one's satisfaction and self-esteem. As couples engage less in face-to-face interactions and more in digital dialogues, the quality of emotional connection can suffer. This qualitative shift raises questions about the long-term viability of relationships nurtured primarily through virtual spaces, as individuals struggle with authenticity and vulnerability in a world dominated by filters and highlights. In addition to these challenges, the proliferation of social media undeniably offers unique opportunities for enhancing relationship dynamics, enabling users to build connections that transcend geographical boundaries. Social platforms allow individuals to interact with potential partners from diverse backgrounds, fostering a sense of community among like-minded individuals. This broadening of social horizons can lead to deeper understanding and appreciation of different cultures, ultimately enriching personal relationships. Many couples report that social media provides an avenue for maintaining contact and intimacy, especially in long-distance relationships where physical proximity is compromised. The ability to share experiences and moments in real-time through photos or videos can help sustain a sense of togetherness despite the distance. To maximize these benefits, users must navigate the complexities of digital interaction wisely, fostering an environment that promotes genuine connection while steering clear of the superficial traps that can dilute the richness of relationship-building in the digital age.

# The Blurring of Lines Between Friendship and Dating

Navigating the space between friendship and romantic interest has become increasingly complex in todays digital world. Social media and dating platforms blur the lines of these relationships, allowing individuals to connect in multifaceted ways. Friendships, often built on shared interests and foundations of trust, can take on a romantic tone when individuals engage in more intimate forms of communication. The ease with which people can express themselves through texts and social media posts lends to a unique dynamic, where platonic feelings can evolve into romantic possibilities. In many cases, this dynamic creates situationships, where neither party is fully committed to defining their bond, leaving them both in a state of uncertainty. By failing to establish clear intentions, individuals navigate a precarious path that often leads to confusion, jealousy, and disappointment. Instinctively, humans crave connection, and the digital age has not only heightened this longing but also modified it. The proliferation of dating apps encourages the notion that relationships can be instantaneously formed based on surface-level attributes, such as appearance and likes. This shift toward superficial assessment can dilute the deeper attributes often present in friendships, like emotional support and shared life experiences. A friendship can transition into romance over time as individuals become more comfortable and vulnerable with each other. When dating is intermingled with friendship, the stakes elevate, introducing the possibility of heartbreak should romantic feelings not be reciprocated. What starts as a light-hearted friendship can swiftly turn complicated, challenging individuals to navigate their expectations and feelings more carefully than they may have been accustomed to doing in previous generations. As individuals venture deeper into the complexities of relationships in the digital age, understanding the distinctions between friendship and romantic interest becomes paramount. Increased transparency in communication may alleviate some of the tension surrounding evolving relationships. Discussing intentions openly can prevent misunderstandings and foster a more organic progression whether they remain friends or evolve into something more significant. Recognizing that the boundaries often overlap can provide clarity for individuals attempting to traverse this new relational landscape. Reassessing the value of friendship in the face of romantic interest could lead to more profound connections. By appreciating the solid foundation established through friendship, individuals might find that such a base can contribute to healthier, more resilient romantic partnerships in the long run.

# XX. MYTH: ONLINE DATING IS A LAST RESORT

In contemporary society, the stigma surrounding online dating is primarily rooted in outdated perceptions that categorize it as a desperate measure for those unable to find love through traditional avenues. This viewpoint overlooks the significant evolution of online dating platforms, which have become increasingly sophisticated and widely accepted. Users range from young professionals looking for meaningful connections to older individuals seeking companionship, demonstrating that these platforms cater to a diverse audience. The data shows that millions engage on these sites not because they lack options, but because they seek to expand their dating horizons in an increasingly busy world. By leveraging technology, many find it easier to meet others who share similar interests and values, thereby facilitating deeper connections that may not occur in conventional social settings. Misconceptions about online dating as a fallback option overlook its capacity to enhance romantic possibilities with unprecedented efficiency. Research indicates that many users of dating applications actively choose this approach as a primary means of meeting potential partners rather than a last-resort strategy. Online platforms empower individuals to curate their dating experiences, allowing them to communicate preferences and establish relationships based on mutual interests. The algorithms employed by these services actively facilitate connections, often leading to relationships that may not have developed in offline environments. The anonymity and broader selection available through these sites can reduce the pressures associated with first interactions, providing users with a more comfortable setting to engage and explore potential matches. The narrative that online dating represents a last resort is increasingly being marginalized as the growing number of success stories challenges this belief. Considerable evidence from various studies reveals that couples who meet through online dating are just as likely, if not more so, to form long-term relationships and marriages as those who meet in traditional ways. This trend reflects a shift in societal attitudes, where online dating is now embraced as a legitimate and effective means of finding love. By debunking the myth that digital romance is a desperate endeavor, it becomes clear that these platforms can serve as valuable tools for many in the quest for genuine connections, allowing users to navigate the complexities of modern relationships with greater ease, intent, and purpose.

## Stigmas Surrounding Online Dating

Despite the growing acceptance of online dating, lingering stigmas continue to affect how individuals perceive and engage with these platforms. Historically, online dating has been associated with desperation or failure to find meaningful connections through traditional means. Many believe that those who turn to dating apps are simply unable to attract partners in person, leading to an unfair labeling of users as socially inept or incapable of romance. This stereotype can create a barrier for individuals who genuinely seek connections through digital avenues, further reinforcing the stigma. As a result, the apprehension surrounding online dating can dissuade potential users from exploring these platforms, limiting their chances of finding fulfilling relationships. This stigma not only hinders personal experiences but can also perpetuate the belief that online love lacks

authenticity or depth, overshadowing the experiences of countless couples who have successfully met and formed lasting partnerships through these services. Concerns around the authenticity of online connections add another layer to the stigmas associated with digital dating. Many individuals fear that profiles
are often misleading, showcasing idealized versions of users
that bear little resemblance to reality. The prevalence of curated
photos and embellished bios may foster distrust, reinforcing the
belief that online romance is inherently superficial. This skepticism can make dating platform users wary of developing deeper
connections, as they may question the motives and true intentions of those they encounter. The pressures of constant engagement and instant gratification can exacerbate this issue, causing
individuals to pursue fleeting romances rather than fostering
genuine emotional bonds. While many users navigate these digital encounters with caution, the fear of deception and superficiality ultimately perpetuates a cycle of skepticism around the
efficacy of online dating, which can deter potential users from
embracing the opportunities these platforms present. Addressing these stigmas requires a collective effort to normalize and
destigmatize online dating as a legitimate means of finding
love. Education plays a pivotal role in reshaping perceptions;
initiatives that highlight success stories and the diverse reasons
individuals utilize dating apps could greatly diminish negative
stereotypes. Encouraging open conversations about online dating experiences can also serve to validate those who seek partnerships through digital means, showcasing the positive potential of these platforms. By promoting a balanced view that recognizes both the advantages and challenges of online dating,
society can cultivate a more accepting environment where

individuals feel empowered to share their experiences without fear of judgment. Dismantling these stigmas is crucial for allowing individuals to explore their romantic options freely and assist in reconceptualizing online dating as a genuine avenue for forming meaningful connections.

## Changing Perceptions of Online Platforms

In recent years, societal attitudes toward online dating platforms have shifted markedly, moving from skepticism to acceptance. Initially regarded as mechanisms for the lonely or desperate, these platforms are now recognized as legitimate avenues for exploring romantic relationships. This transformation can be attributed to the normalization of digital interactions across various aspects of life, including work and social communications. As people became more comfortable with online interactions, the stigma surrounding online dating diminished, allowing for broader demographic participation. A growing body of research indicates that many individuals experience success in finding meaningful connections through these platforms, further enhancing their credibility as a viable method for meeting potential partners. The promise of algorithms tailoring matches according to user preferences is a significant contributor to the evolving perceptions of online dating. Many platforms utilize sophisticated algorithms to analyze user data, ostensibly increasing the likelihood of compatibility between matched individuals. As users engage with these technologies, they often find themselves more open to the idea of online dating as an efficient means of expanding their romantic options. The reliance on algorithms also raises questions about the simplicity of human connection. The tendency to equate numerical compatibility with romantic potential can lead to disillusionment when real-life interactions do not align with the expectations set by digital profiles. While algorithms may enhance user experience, they also risk oversimplifying the dynamic and nuanced nature of personal relationships. The journey toward understanding and utilizing online dating platforms requires a nuanced approach that goes beyond surface-level engagement. As users navigate these spaces, they must remain vigilant not only about their own motives but also about the constructed nature of online personas. The allure of immediate connections can often overshadow the importance of developing genuine relationships. Consequently, individuals are encouraged to adopt more critical perspectives when using these platforms, recognizing that behind every curated profile lies a complex human being with an intricate emotional landscape. By promoting a balanced understanding of online interactions, individuals can foster healthier engagements, allowing for authentic connections that challenge the prevalent myths and superficialities often associated with dating in the digital age.

## The Normalization of Online Dating

In recent years, an increasing number of individuals have turned to digital platforms as a primary means of finding romantic partners. This shift reflects changing social norms where meeting potential mates through traditional avenues—such as mutual friends or social gatherings—has become less common. Online dating allows users to explore a vast pool of potential matches from the comfort of their homes, transcending geographical constraints and enabling connections that may not have been possible otherwise. The growing acceptance of these platforms signifies a broader cultural transition toward digital interactions being recognized as legitimate and practical ways to forge meaningful relationships. The convenience and efficiency of online dating often appeal to busy individuals who struggle to find time for traditional dating methods. Modern dating apps and websites employ sophisticated algorithms designed to enhance user experience by analyzing preferences and behaviors to match users effectively. While this technology promises to streamline the dating process and increase the likelihood of finding a compatible partner, it also raises concerns regarding the authenticity of the connections formed. Users may become overly reliant on these algorithms, which can lead to superficial assessments of compatibility, based on limited information such as photos and brief bios. This reliance may foster a sense of disengagement from genuine emotional connections, as individuals often succumb to the temptation to swipe for convenience rather than taking the time to foster deeper interactions. The nature of digital interactions can inadvertently encourage users to present idealized versions of themselves, contributing to disillusionment when real-life meetings do not align with online portrayals. Despite the pitfalls that accompany online dating, the advantages it offers often outweigh the negatives, particularly in terms of reaching a diverse audience. Many individuals find that they can explore romantic possibilities far beyond their immediate social circles, which can lead to more enriching relationships. This broadened scope allows users to move past geographical boundaries, potentially introducing them to partners with varied backgrounds, interests, and life experiences. It is crucial for users to approach these platforms with a balanced perspective. Understanding that while online dating provides opportunities, it is not a guaranteed pathway to romance helps mitigate unrealistic expectations. Encouraging users to view their digital dating experiences as just one component of the broader spectrum of romantic exploration can ultimately lead to more fulfilling connections and the dismantling of the myths surrounding simple, algorithm-driven match making.

# XXI. TRUTH: THE IMPORTANCE OF SELF-REFLECTION

The act of self-reflection plays a critical role in understanding personal values and emotional needs, particularly in the context of online dating. Many individuals enter the digital dating sphere with a predetermined notion of their ideal partner, often heavily influenced by societal norms and expectations. Engaging in self-reflection encourages individuals to question these assumptions. By examining past relationships and interactions, users can gain insights into what truly matters to them, beyond superficial traits such as looks or social media appeal. Through this reflective process, individuals can better articulate their desires and establish healthier relationship standards, ultimately enhancing their likelihood of finding a true match. This introspection allows for a deeper awareness of personal vulnerabilities and strengths, promoting authenticity in profiles and interactions while journeying through the often chaotic landscape of online connections. Knowledge of one's values and emotional states is further crucial in navigating the minefield of potential misrepresentations that could surface in online dating. Users frequently encounter profiles that present an exaggerated version of reality, to the extent that what starts as a mere physical attraction can lead to unrealistic expectations. When individuals engage in thorough self-examination, they cultivate an ability to discern authenticity in others. As a result, they are less likely to fall prey to the superficial charm of misleading profiles. Matching with others becomes less about maintaining an illusion of perfection and more about forming genuine connections that align with ones true self. This awareness not only fosters more meaningful interactions but also cultivates resilience against disappointment, as users approach potential matches with a balanced understanding of their motivations and expectations. The importance of self-reflection transcends the mere act of finding love by fostering emotional maturity and resilience. In a dating environment flooded with algorithmic-driven matches and instant gratification, the necessity for individuals to pause and reflect is magnified. By setting aside time for introspection, users can ensure that they are not only seeking a partner that fulfills a momentary desire but rather one who aligns with their deeper values and interests. This reflective approach encourages patience and clarity, allowing individuals to navigate the ups and downs of online dating with a clearer sense of purpose. Consequently, the pursuit of romantic connections transitions from superficial interactions to meaningful engagements, empowering individuals to find love that is grounded in truth and mutual understanding.

## Understanding Personal Goals in Dating

Defining personal goals in dating is essential for understanding ones motivations and desires when venturing into the realm of romantic relationships, especially in a landscape dominated by digital interaction. Individuals often enter dating platforms with various aspirations, ranging from casual encounters to seeking long-term commitments. These goals can significantly influence how one engages with others, shaping the selection of potential partners and the nature of communication. Individuals who take the time to articulate their desires are more likely to attract compatible matches. Clear expectations help to minimize disappointment and enhance the overall experience, ultimately fostering healthier relationships. Hence, the importance of self-reflection prior to engaging with dating apps cannot be overstated, as it allows users to assess their emotional readiness and clarify what they ultimately seek. While personal goals in dating can serve as guiding principles, they can also inadvertently lead to unrealistic expectations. The digital dating landscape often promotes a phenomenon where users are dazzled by an overwhelming number of choices, leading to a paradox of choice that can diminish satisfaction. As individuals sift through profiles with striking images and captivating bios, the inherent risks of superficiality become apparent. Users may find themselves prioritizing physical appearance or superficial traits over deeper compatibility factors such as values, interests, and life goals. This tendency can result in shallow connections that fade quickly or, conversely, the pursuit of idealized partners based on filtered versions of reality. Understanding this dynamic encourages users to approach online dating with discernment, balancing personal goals with an awareness of how digital impressions can distort genuine connections. Articulating and reassessing personal goals in dating is an ongoing process, particularly after interactions with potential partners occur. These encounters serve as opportunities for individuals to learn about not only themselves but also about what qualities they truly value in a partner. Feedback from these experiences can inform future decisions, allowing individuals to refine their criteria and grow emotionally. As trends in online dating evolve, users must remain adaptable in their approach, being open to the idea that goals may shift over time. Whether it's moving from a casual dating mindset to seeking a serious relationship, being aware of ones changing intentions can make the dating journey more fruitful and fulfilling. Continuous self-evaluation ultimately empowers individuals to cultivate connections that resonate with their evolving desires, fostering the potential for deeper, more authentic relationships in an increasingly complex digital age.

## The Role of Self-Awareness

Understanding one's own inner landscape plays a fundamental role in navigating the complex world of online dating. In an environment characterized by rapid connections and superficial assessments, self-awareness facilitates more meaningful engagement. By reflecting on personal motivations for seeking love, an individual can develop clearer intentions, moving beyond mere attraction to cultivating deeper relationships. This understanding serves as a protective mechanism against the impulsivity that often accompanies online interactions, where the lure of instant gratification can blur judgment. Individuals who recognize patterns in their past relationships may avoid repeating mistakes, thereby enhancing their chances of forming healthier connections. Thus, self-awareness empowers users to approach online dating with intentionality, leading to choices that align with their true desires rather than external pressures or fleeting desires. Self-awareness cultivates resilience in the face of the inevitable challenges that come with online dating. Rejection is a common occurrence in these virtual landscapes, but a strong sense of self can mitigate its negative impact. When individuals are conscious of their self-worth and understand that rejection is often not a reflection of their value, they are better equipped to cope with the emotional fallout. This clarity can lead to a more grounded approach to dating, where individuals view each interaction as a learning experience rather than a definitive judgment on their identity. Self-aware individuals are more inclined to communicate authentically in their profiles and conversations. By presenting their true selves rather than a curated facade, they increase the likelihood of attracting compatible partners who resonate with their genuine personality. In addition to fostering emotional resilience and authentic communication, self-awareness aids in recognizing and respecting personal boundaries. In the world of online dating, where interactions can swiftly escalate, understanding one's limits is crucial. Being aware of what one is willing to compromise on in a relationship, as well as identifying non-negotiable values, allows individuals to engage in dating more thoughtfully. This clarity not only prevents potential heartache but also encourages healthier boundaries in new connections. Someone aware of their comfort zones might avoid sharing intimate details too soon or recognize when a conversation veers into uncomfortable territory. Cultivating self-awareness is indispensable for online dating success, creating a foundation that supports emotional health, authentic engagement, and personal integrity.

## Evaluating Relationship Readiness

Recognizing and assessing personal values and emotional maturity is crucial for determining relationship readiness. Individuals need to reflect on their priorities, such as personal goals, career aspirations, and family values, to understand how these elements may affect a partnership. Emotional maturity encompasses the ability to recognize and manage one's feelings and to empathize with others' emotions. A person who possesses emotional resilience is more likely to communicate openly and address potential conflicts constructively. Consequently, self-awareness and emotional intelligence act as foundations for healthy interaction in romantic relationships, helping individuals navigate the complexities of love. By taking the time to engage in self-reflection, potential partners can identify what they want from a relationship, which in turn leads to more fulfilling and purposeful connections online. The significance of external factors, such as social life and support systems, represents another critical element in evaluating readiness for a romantic relationship. Strong friendships and a supportive family can provide a safety net that enhances an individual's emotional well-being. Having a solid foundation of social support allows individuals to feel secure in pursuing new relationships, as they know they can rely on their existing connections during times of transition or uncertainty. An active social life can offer valuable insights into interpersonal dynamics and relationship norms, helping individuals learn what works and what does not in a partnership. Thus, an understanding of one's social environment and the quality of existing relationships can serve as essential indicators of whether someone is in a suitable place to embark on an online dating journey. Preparation for the potential challenges of dating, particularly in a digital context, is essential for assessing relationship readiness. Understanding that online dating can entail a unique set of hurdles, such as miscommunication, misrepresentation, and varying levels of commitment, allows individuals to mentally and emotionally prepare for these complexities. A proactive approach to setting boundaries and determining personal comfort levels can contribute significantly to a positive online dating experience. By acknowledging the realities of this landscape, individuals can more readily equip themselves with coping strategies and realistic expectations. Emphasizing the importance of flexibility and open-mindedness will enhance personal growth and adaptability during the dating process, ultimately leading to deeper and more meaningful connections that outlive superficial interactions fostered by technology.

# XXII. MYTH: YOU CAN'T FIND TRUE LOVE ONLINE

The landscape of modern romance has evolved significantly with the advent of online dating, challenging long-held beliefs about love and connection. One prevalent misconception is that it is impossible to find genuine love through digital platforms. Despite this skepticism, research increasingly suggests that online dating can be a legitimate avenue for meaningful relationships. Many individuals have shared success stories of finding lasting partnerships through these channels, attesting to the feasibility of forming authentic connections online. The intricate algorithms designed to match users based on shared interests and compatibility can actually enhance the chances of meeting someone truly compatible, countering the myth that online dating lacks depth. The anonymity of online platforms allows individuals to express themselves more freely, often leading to deeper conversations that might not occur in traditional settings. In addition to the potential for authentic emotional connections, the vast array of dating platforms available today caters to diverse preferences and lifestyles. Niche dating sites focus on specific interests or communities, helping users connect based on shared values and beliefs. This specialization enhances the likelihood of finding someone who aligns with one's personal philosophies, thereby challenging the idea that online interactions are inherently superficial. Studies highlight that users of online dating platforms often report higher satisfaction rates in their relationships compared to those who meet through conventional means. This success speaks to the ability of these platforms to facilitate deeper engagement and connection, bridging gaps that might exist in one's immediate social circles while debunking the belief that such environments only foster fleeting encounters devoid of emotional significance. It is essential to recognize, however, that while online dating can indeed lead to genuine love, it also demands a discerning approach. Users must remain vigilant about the potential for misrepresentation, as profiles can sometimes present idealized versions of individuals rather than their true selves. As such, while it is possible to forge meaningful connections online, these relationships can also be fraught with challenges that require careful navigation. Being mindful of the risks associated with superficial impressions is crucial for users seeking to avoid disappointment. Thus, a balanced perspective on online dating promotes an understanding that, while true love can certainly be found through these platforms, it is imperative to approach them with both hope and caution, empowering individuals to cultivate authentic relationships amidst the complexities of today's digital dating landscape.

## Stereotypes About Online Relationships

Common misconceptions about online relationships frequently stem from a lack of understanding regarding the complexities of digital interactions. Many individuals hold the belief that relationships formed online are inherently less valid or meaningful than those established in traditional settings. This stereotype marginalizes the emotional and psychological investment that online partners can have in their relationships. Studies have shown that individuals who meet through online platforms often engage in deep conversations and meaningful exchanges that can foster strong connections. Contrary to stereotypes suggesting that online daters are merely seeking casual interactions, these platforms can facilitate the development of profound emotional bonds that rival those formed in face-to-face encounters. As such, it is essential to recognize that the mode of meeting does not determine the depth or authenticity of the relationship. Contrary to prevailing stereotypes, the demographics of online dating participants reveal a diverse landscape that contradicts the notion of it being a last resort for the socially awkward. Data shows that a broad spectrum of individuals utilizes these platforms, ranging from young adults seeking casual relationships to older individuals looking for meaningful partnerships. This demographic shift illustrates that online dating is increasingly seen as a legitimate avenue for finding love, rather than a refuge for those lacking social skills. The use of technology-based matchmaking allows users to curate their dating experiences based on preferences, interests, and compatibility metrics. This democratization of dating means that more people can find matches that resonate with them, challenging the notion that online connections are superficial or limited to specific niches of society. The stereotype that online relationships lack authenticity often overlooks the methods by which individuals navigate these digital platforms. Many users approach online dating with a deliberate strategy, taking significant care in crafting their profiles and selecting the platforms that best align with their relationship goals. This intent can lead to more authentic and genuine interactions, as potential partners are often upfront about their desires and intentions. The pressure to present an idealized version of oneself can lead to disillusionment when the reality of a relationship unfolds. By understanding the nuances of how online dating works, including the balancing act between self-presentation and authenticity, individuals can refine their expectations and approach. Shifting perspectives on online relationships can dissolve the stereotypes that shroud them, promoting a more nuanced understanding of what it means to find love in the digital age.

## Success Rates of Online Relationships

There is a significant emphasis on the short-term and immediate gratification that online dating offers, yet such instant connections often compromise the depth of relationships. Users frequently become captivated by the enticing prospects of abundance—an endless array of potential partners at their fingertips. This abundance can lead to a paradox of choice, wherein too many options may induce anxiety and hinder decision-making. Research indicates that individuals who engage in online dating might become accustomed to superficial criteria when evaluating potential partners, prioritizing profiles and images over emotional compatibility. Consequently, many relationships that begin online may lack the substantive foundations necessary for long-term success. While establishing connections through digital platforms can lead to romance, a reliance on initial attraction governed by fleeting impressions often means that deeper emotional bonds remain underdeveloped. The success rates of online relationships are deeply intertwined with user intentions and expectations. While many people enter the digital dating landscape seeking meaningful connections, others are primarily motivated by casual encounters or validation. An investigation into the motivations behind why individuals choose online dating reveals a spectrum ranging from the desire for genuine companionship to an escape from loneliness. Success, therefore, is not merely measured by the number of matches or dates secured but rather by the fulfillment and happiness derived from those interactions. Couples who report higher satisfaction often emphasize their commitment to effective communication and shared values. Consequently, the definition of success in online relationships must be multi-faceted, encompassing not only the establishment of a connection but also the nurturing of that bond through mutual understanding and respect. It is essential to recognize that online relationships are influenced by various external factors, including societal expectations and personal circumstances. The stigma surrounding online dating has diminished over the years, with many now considering it a legitimate avenue for finding love. This shift in perception can significantly impact an individuals confidence and willingness to engage in online platforms. It is vital to navigate these spaces with caution and reflect on personal values and goals. Couples who embrace transparency and authenticity in their online interactions are often better equipped to manage potential pitfalls, such as misrepresentation or ghosting. By fostering an environment where honesty thrives, users can enhance the likelihood of developing relationships that stand the test of time. Understanding the dynamics of online dating requires a mindfulness that balances hope with realism, allowing individuals to cultivate meaningful connections amidst the digital landscape.

## Real-Life Examples of Lasting Love

Amid the complexities of modern romance facilitated by online platforms, enduring relationships serve as poignant reminders of loves potential. Take, for instance, the story of John and Mary, who met through a dating app in their mid-thirties. The initial attraction stemmed from their shared interests in literature and travel, but what has solidified their bond over the years is a deep-seated commitment to communication and mutual support. They regularly engage in activities that fortify their connection, such as weekly date nights and engaging in open discussions about their goals and emotions. Their journey illustrates that while online encounters can set the stage for romance, it is the consistent nurturing of the relationship that leads toward lasting love, transcending the quick fix culture that often characterizes digital dating. Equally compelling are the stories of couples who have successfully transitioned from digital interaction to lifelong companionship. Consider the narrative of Alex and Jamie, who navigated the early stages of their relationship primarily through video calls during the pandemic. This unique beginning forced them to deepen their emotional intimacy before ever meeting in person, as they relied on meaningful conversations rather than physical attraction alone. By sharing their vulnerabilities and aspirations, they constructed a robust foundation that ultimately withstood the pressures that emerge from transitioning to shared living spaces. Their experience demonstrates that the strength of a relationship can often be magnified when couples prioritize emotional connection over superficial engagement, illuminating the profound potential for love to flourish, even in less conventional circumstances. The tale of older couples re-entering the dating scene adds another layer of depth to our understanding of lasting love. Take, for example, Susan and Bob, both in their sixties, who discovered each other through an online community for seniors. Their journey embodies resilience as they navigated the trials of previous relationships and the challenges of dating later in life. With a shared appreciation for lifes simpler joys, they emphasize companionship and mutual care over societal perceptions of romantic standards. The lessons learned from their experiences reveal that deep emotional bonds can flourish at any age, challenging the myth that romantic fulfillment is exclusive to youth. Their relationship exemplifies how online platforms can serve as avenues for authentic connections, showcasing that love, when rooted in kindness and respect, is truly ageless.

# XXIII. TRUTH: THE FUTURE OF ONLINE DATING

The impact of technology on the dynamics of modern relationships is profound, particularly as online dating continues to flourish. Algorithms, designed to analyze user preferences and behaviors, shape the matchmaking process, promising potential partners based on compatibility scores rather than genuine human connection. This reliance on technology can lead to a superficial understanding of romance, as individuals may become more focused on data metrics than emotional resonance. The ease of access to countless profiles fosters a culture of instant gratification, where users often overlook deeper connections in favor of quick matches. As users navigate this digital landscape, it is crucial to balance algorithmic recommendations with a conscious effort to engage authentically, moving beyond the surface-level connections generated by these platforms. The allure of online dating can sometimes mask the complexities inherent in developing meaningful relationships. Often, the narratives presented through profiles and photographs can be misleading, crafted to appeal to potential matches rather than reflecting true personalities. This distortion of truth creates a treacherous terrain for seekers of love, where emotional investment may be based on curated, rather than authentic, representations. The ease of creating false identities or portraying exaggerated versions of oneself complicates the trust factor that is foundational in any relationship. Users must consequently be discerning, fostering skills to read between the lines of digital narratives, as well as to articulate their own truths without succumbing to the temptation of embellishment. Addressing these challenges requires a commitment to honesty and transparency, which are indispensable in navigating the future of online dating. The evolution of online dating platforms presents a dual-edged sword, offering both expansive opportunities and inherent risks. As these services continue to diversify and adapt to user demands, they have the potential to cultivate genuine connections among individuals who might not have crossed paths otherwise. Neglecting the realities of human interaction can lead to disillusionment and frustration. The pursuit of meaningful relationships in a digital era necessitates a more nuanced understanding of human emotions and motivations behind online profiles. By adopting a mindful approach to online dating, users can better appreciate the distinctions between love and infatuation, allowing for a more informed and fulfilling romantic journey. Embracing the truth—both in oneself and in others—will play a pivotal role in shaping the future of love in the digital age, steering individuals towards a deeper understanding of their desires and connections.

## Emerging Trends in Online Dating

The landscape of online dating has undergone significant transformation in recent years, driven largely by shifts in societal attitudes and technological innovations. A growing number of platforms now cater to niche markets, allowing individuals to connect over shared interests and life experiences rather than just superficial characteristics like physical appearance. Apps focusing on specific demographics or lifestyles, such as veganism or LGBTQ+ communities, have emerged to provide users with tailored experiences that resonate with their values. This trend reflects a broader desire for authenticity and deeper connections, as users often seek meaningful relationships over transient encounters. The emergence of video dating options allows individuals to engage in more personal interactions before meeting in person, thereby reducing the impression of superficiality frequently associated with traditional text-based dating. Another noteworthy trend is the integration of artificial intelligence and machine learning into dating platforms. These algorithms not only optimize match suggestions based on user preferences but also analyze behaviors to enhance the overall matching process. Such technology can increase the likelihood of compatible matches by evaluating factors like communication styles, interests, and even emotional compatibility. This wave of algorithm-driven dating raises important questions about the limitations and ethics surrounding technological mediation in human relationships. While some users embrace this sophisticated approach to finding love, others find the reliance on algorithms troubling, as it prioritizes data over genuine human interaction, potentially reducing complex individuals to mere data points. It is crucial for users to remain aware of the intricate balance between technology and the nuanced nature of human connections as they navigate these platforms. The increasing normalization of online dating also brings forth significant cultural and psychological implications. Societal perceptions are shifting, with online dating becoming more accepted as a legitimate avenue for finding partners, yet this shift may create unrealistic expectations. As success stories flood social media feed, individuals might develop the illusion that finding love online is both effortless and instantaneous. This phenomenon can lead to frustration and disappointment among users who fail to achieve instant chemistry or who encounter multiple unsuccessful interactions. Consequently, it becomes essential for users to temper their expectations and approach online dating with a mindful perspective, recognizing that it is a tool for connection rather than a guarantee of romance. As users cultivate a more realistic understanding of the online dating landscape, they can navigate these platforms with greater resilience, enhancing their chances of forming meaningful relationships while also safeguarding their emotional well-being.

## Technological Innovations Impacting Dating

The landscape of dating has dramatically shifted, presenting both opportunities and challenges for modern romantics. One significant technological innovation is the use of algorithms in matchmaking systems found on dating platforms. These algorithms analyze user data, preferences, and behaviors to suggest potential matches that align closely with individual profiles. While on the surface this appears efficient, creating the illusion of a perfect partner just a few clicks away, the reliance on such technology raises numerous questions. Critics argue that these algorithms can perpetuate biases by filtering out diverse options and prioritizing certain traits over others. Consequently, users may become ensnared in echo chambers where their preferences limit their exposure to a broader spectrum of potential partners. Thus, while algorithms can enhance the online dating experience by offering personalized suggestions, they simultaneously risk fostering a more superficial approach to romance, where genuine connection may be overshadowed by data-driven projections. Another noteworthy innovation reshaping the dating scene is the rise of mobile dating applications. These platforms leverage the connectivity of smartphones to allow constant access to potential matches, significantly altering how people engage in romantic pursuits. The allure of swiping right or left creates a fast-paced environment that promotes immediacy; users often feel compelled to make quick decisions based on surface-level attributes. This can lead to a perception that relationships are merely a series of transactions, rather than meaningful connections. The omnipresence of mobile technology introduces the phenomenon of paradox of choice, where an overwhelming number of options can lead to anxiety and indecision rather than satisfaction. As users navigate this fast-paced space, many find themselves questioning the depth of their connections, leading to a potential deterioration of relationship quality as well as increased instances of ghosting and superficial interactions. Despite these innovations, there remains a critical need to cultivate authenticity within the online dating environment. The allure of projecting an idealized self through curated profiles can often distort reality, resulting in misrepresentation and disappointment during in-person meetings. Users may present themselves through selectively chosen photos and polished bios that fail to capture their true essence. This phenomenon not only contributes to individual discontent but also undermines the foundations of trust essential for any budding relationship. To counteract these trends, it is imperative for users to approach online dating with a mindset geared towards sincerity and openness. By being candid about their true selves and engaging with potential partners thoughtfully, individuals can foster deeper and more meaningful connections. The onus lies with users to transcend the superficial tendencies promoted by technology, allowing for richer relational dynamics capable of thriving in the modern dating landscape.

## Predictions for the Future Landscape

As the digital landscape continues to evolve, so too does the way individuals engage with dating apps and platforms. The future of online dating is likely to be shaped significantly by advancements in technology, particularly artificial intelligence and machine learning. These technologies are expected to refine algorithms that facilitate user matching based on compatibility factors far beyond mere interests or physical attraction. By analyzing user behavior and feedback, future dating platforms may achieve a more nuanced understanding of what constitutes a successful pairing, thus minimizing the superficial engagements that currently plague many existing services. Enhanced AI could lead to more meaningful connections by curating personalized experiences that resonate with users emotional and relational needs rather than focusing solely on simplistic metrics. The normalization of virtual reality and augmented reality within the dating sphere presents an intriguing dimension to the future of relationship formation. With VR and AR technology becoming more accessible, users may soon have the opportunity to engage in immersive dating experiences, such as virtual dates in idyllic settings or interactive activities that simulate shared experiences. This shift could revolutionize how people perceive intimacy and connection, reducing the anxiety often associated with first meetings. As these platforms gain traction, they may inspire a cultural shift towards embracing more creative and dynamic forms of interaction, fostering deeper emotional bonds that transcend the visual judgments often cast in traditional online dating. Consequently, the potential for genuine connection could increase, redefining what it means to meet someone in the digital age. In addressing safety and authenticity, the future of online dating will likely place greater emphasis on user verification and accountability. As concerns about catfishing and deceptive profiles persist, platforms may implement stricter verification processes, such as biometric identification or extensive background checks, to bolster user trust. This shift could mitigate some of the skepticism surrounding online dating, encouraging a culture of honesty and transparency. Users are predicted to become more discerning in their engagement, seeking platforms that prioritize ethical practices over mere profitability. Increased scrutiny may lead to the development of communities that advocate for healthier dating practices, emphasizing mutual respect and consent as foundational principles. In effect, the evolving landscape may cultivate a space in which authenticity and safety are paramount, thereby enhancing the overall experience of seeking love in the digital age.

# XXIV. STRATEGIES FOR SUCCESSFUL ONLINE DATING

Developing a compelling and genuine online profile is paramount to successful dating in the digital realm. Crafting a well-rounded biography involves highlighting personality traits, interests, and values, rather than merely listing hobbies or preferences. This authentic portrayal not only attracts like-minded individuals but also sets the stage for deeper connections. The incorporation of high-quality photographs can significantly enhance the allure of a profile. Images should be recent and showcase genuine moments where the individual appears relaxed and happy; this authenticity invites prospective matches to engage more freely. By placing emphasis on what makes one unique, users can encourage potential partners to see beyond the superficial and forge authentic connections right from the start. A thoughtfully presented profile serves as a foundation for meaningful interactions, widening the scope of suitable matches and reducing the likelihood of misunderstandings early on. Effective communication is another cornerstone of success in the online dating landscape. Upon initiating contact, it is essential to maintain a balance between enthusiasm and curiosity while avoiding overwhelming the other party. Open-ended questions facilitate conversations and allow for personal exploration, enabling users to uncover common interests and shared values. Reflective listening, where one actively engages with the responses given, not only demonstrates genuine interest but also fosters a sense of intimacy even through the digital medium. It is crucial to be mindful of tone and wording, as texts can easily be misinterpreted without the nuances of verbal cues. Setting realistic expectations about responses is equally important, as patience can often yield richer interactions. This form of communication paves the way for building rapport and understanding, ultimately leading to more satisfying and authentic connections. Establishing boundaries and ensuring safety remains a top priority when navigating the world of online dating. Users should prioritize personal safety by refraining from sharing sensitive information prematurely, such as home addresses or financial details, until trust is firmly established. It is advisable to suggest public spaces for initial meet-ups, which not only promotes safety but also eases the pressure typical of first encounters. Cultivating awareness of red flags, such as inconsistencies in a partner's story or overly secretive behavior, can help individuals make informed decisions regarding potential matches. Developing a sense of self-worth and confidence in ones dating journey is equally critical. By recognizing that rejection is a natural part of online dating, users can approach interactions with resilience, enabling them to navigate the complexities with greater ease. Adopting these strategies creates a more balanced and secure online dating experience, enhancing the chances of finding meaningful connections.

## Crafting an Authentic Profile

A carefully crafted profile serves as the digital footprint of one's personality in the realm of online dating; it is the initial impression that can shape a potential connection. Notably, authenticity plays a pivotal role in this process, as users often seek companions who reflect their values and interests. When individuals compose their profiles, they should prioritize honesty over embellishment, resisting the urge to conform to an idealized version of themselves. Claims in research indicate that profiles show-casing genuine attributes—personal anecdotes, nuanced hob-bies, or unique experiences—tend to attract like-minded indi-viduals. This authenticity cultivates the groundwork for mean-ingful interactions, as potential matches are more likely to en-gage with profiles that resonate with their own identities. At the core of this endeavor lies the understanding that a well-bal-anced portrayal not only aids in finding suitable matches but also fosters a sense of connectivity that transcends the superfi-cial nature often associated with online encounters. In addition to authenticity, the presentation of information plays a crucial role in shaping a profiles efficacy. Engaging language and thoughtful organization can enhance the appeal of a dating pro-file, making it more inviting for readers. Profile creators should aim for a blend of relatability and intrigue, ensuring that their texts highlight personality without overwhelming potential matches. Artistic choices, such as the selection of photographs or tagline crafting, can profoundly impact a user's first impres-sion. According to studies in social psychology, visuals have a significant bearing on attraction; therefore, choosing images that reflect genuine moments—like hobbies or social gather-ings—can create a more compelling narrative. Carefully chosen words that resonate with the intended audience further contrib-ute to the profiles ability to convey ones essence effectively. A polished yet sincere portrayal is essential to navigating the com-plexities of online dating while retaining a sense of individuality. The interplay between digital identity and real-world connec-tions raises vital questions about the sustainability of relation-ships initiated through online platforms. While an authentic pro-file can initially spark interest and foster connections, it is crucial that users remain mindful of the need for continuous alignment between their online personas and their true selves. As interactions evolve from virtual discussions to actual meetings, discrepancies between depicted and genuine personas can lead to disillusionment and distrust. Psychological research underscores the importance of vulnerability and genuine communication in establishing intimacy, indicating that the authenticity of the online profile must extend to real life for lasting connections. Users should embrace the process of authenticity not only in their profiles but throughout their interactions, as this approach promotes transparency, encourages deeper connections, and reduces the likelihood of false expectations. Crafting an authentic profile isnt merely a marketing strategy; it represents the foundational step in navigating the complexities of online love, advocating for integrity beyond the screen.

## Effective Communication Techniques

In the evolving landscape of online dating, mastering effective communication techniques is critical for building meaningful connections. The ability to convey thoughts and feelings clearly is paramount, especially when interactions are mediated by screens. One practical strategy involves active listening, a skill that requires the individual to engage fully in conversations by demonstrating interest and understanding. This can be achieved through affirmative body language, such as nodding, and by summarizing or paraphrasing the other person's points to show comprehension. By validating the emotional content of a conversation, instigators foster a sense of connection that can alleviate the superficiality often associated with online dating profiles. The practice of active listening not only enhances communication but also builds trust, enabling more profound and authentic exchanges between potential partners. Another technique to enhance communication in digital interactions is the intentional use of open-ended questions. Unlike closed questions that prompt simple yes or no responses, open-ended inquiries invite more elaborate responses, encouraging a richer dialogue. Rather than asking, Did you have a good weekend? one might ask, What did you enjoy most about your weekend? This approach encourages the other person to share experiences and feelings, which cultivates a deeper understanding of their personality and values. Incorporating these types of questions helps partners explore common interests, revealing compatibility that extends beyond surface-level attributes. Thus, leveraging open-ended questions serves not just as a conversational tool, but as a foundational method for establishing lasting connections in a digital dating environment that often prioritizes quick interactions over meaningful engagement. The importance of nonverbal cues cannot be overlooked, even in the realm of online communication. Elements such as timing in responses and the use of emojis play an essential role in how messages are perceived and understood. A timely reply can signal interest and engagement, while excessive delays may suggest disinterest or apathy. The strategic use of emojis can enhance emotional expression, providing nuances to text that might otherwise be misinterpreted. Yet, its vital to remain authentic; relying solely on symbols rather than genuine dialogue can hinder deeper understanding. Emphasizing the balance between verbal and nonverbal communication ultimately allows individuals to convey intentions and feelings more effectively, bridging the gap that can often arise in digital interactions. In pursuing sustained and meaningful connections, the integration of these communication techniques may significantly enrich the online dating experience by fostering authenticity and emotional resonance.

## Navigating First Dates Successfully

The initial meeting that occurs between two people can set the tone for future interactions, making the first date a critical juncture in the realm of dating. Preparation is key to navigating this initial encounter successfully; it can be beneficial to choose a location that allows for comfortable conversation, such as a coffee shop or a casual restaurant. This decision not only fosters communication but also eases any anxiety that may arise from the anticipation of a romantic connection. Engaging in light-hearted conversation, focused on shared interests rather than overly personal subjects, can create a relaxed atmosphere, allowing both individuals to feel more at ease. Focusing on body language and maintaining an open demeanor can signal interest and comfort, enhancing the overall experience. A positive first date can pave the way for future interactions by establishing rapport, so investing thought into the setting and conversation is crucial. Another important aspect to consider during a first date is the mutual exchange of personal information, which can either build trust or create discomfort if managed poorly. Its essential to strike a balance between openness and privacy; sharing too little may come across as evasive, while oversharing can make the other person feel overwhelmed. Asking open-ended questions invites the other party to share their thoughts and experiences, thus facilitating deeper connections. Listening attentively not only conveys interest but also helps to gauge whether the chemistry is reciprocal. Discussing conversational boundaries, like topics that may be sensitive or off-limits, demonstrates respect and encourages a comfortable dialogue. By creating a space where both individuals feel free to express themselves, a first date can transcend mere pleasantries and evolve into a meaningful exchange that may lay the groundwork for a potential relationship. In the digital age, where interactions can often morph into superficial exchanges, prioritizing authenticity is essential during first dates. Authenticity fosters a genuine connection that can counteract the often unrealistically curated images presented online. Arriving at a date with an approach that embraces vulnerability can allow for genuine interactions, drawing two individuals together in a way that transcends the idealized versions of themselves. Being transparent about ones online dating background and intentions can mitigate misunderstandings and set the stage for open communication. Instead of striving for perfection or worrying about impressing one another, focusing on authenticity can cultivate a rich and enjoyable experience. This shift in perspective—valuing real connections over digital facades—can yield deeper, more satisfying relationships, encouraging individuals to embrace their true selves and ultimately rediscover the joy of genuine companionship.

# XXV. COMMON MISTAKES TO AVOID IN ONLINE DATING

Navigating the landscape of online dating necessitates an awareness of frequent missteps that can hinder meaningful connections. One of the most significant errors involves neglecting to present an authentic self in dating profiles. Many users, eager to attract attention, curate images or descriptions that are far removed from reality. This not only sets unrealistic expectations but also leads to disappointment and mistrust when these personas clash with actual encounters. Research has indicated that presenting a genuine image—both physically and emotionally—fosters more substantial and lasting connections. Authenticity breeds trust, which is foundational for any relationship, especially one that starts in the digital realm. Embracing one's true self and showcasing personal interests and quirks can enhance the likelihood of attracting a compatible partner who appreciates you for who you are. Another prevalent pitfall in the realm of online dating is the tendency to engage in superficial judgment based solely on profile photographs or brief bios. The instant nature of swiping applications often cultivates an environment where first impressions heavily dictate potential matches. This can lead individuals to overlook deeper compatibility aspects like values, interests, and personality traits. A study conducted by social psychologists highlighted that successful relationships are built on commonalities that extend beyond mere physical attraction. To counteract this superficial tendency, users should take the time to read profiles fully and engage in deeper conversations before making definitive judgments. This can involve asking open-ended questions and sharing personal stories, which can enrich initial interactions and lay a stronger groundwork for future connections. Impatience often disrupts the potential for forming meaningful relationships in online dating. The immediacy of technology encourages users to seek quick gratification, leading many to rush into relationships without adequate vetting or reflection. This eagerness can result in overlooking red flags or ignoring fundamental differences that may pose challenges down the line. Experts recommend pacing oneself and allowing time to cultivate an understanding of prospective partners. Developing patience also allows users to create a richer dating experience, where connections can gradually deepen over time, fostering a sense of security and stability. By understanding the importance of timing and exploration in the digital dating landscape, individuals can cultivate connections that are not just fleeting moments but potentially transformative experiences.

## Pitfalls of Overthinking

In a world where online interactions dominate, individuals often find themselves caught in a web of overanalysis where every message, photo, or profile detail is scrutinized. This relentless tendency to overthink can lead to paralysis by analysis, causing users to miss out on genuine opportunities for connection. Instead of focusing on building relationships, many become ensnared in an endless loop of questioning their intentions, feelings, or the responses they receive. This mental gymnastics not only drains emotional energy but can also lead to false conclusions. A delayed reply might be misinterpreted as disinterest rather than a reflection of the other person's busy life. Thus, overthinking creates unnecessary obstacles that can hinder the potential for meaningful connections, showing a stark contrast to the spontaneity that often characterizes successful relationships. The implications of overthinking in the realm of online dating extend beyond personal frustration; they impact emotional well-being and mental health. An obsession with perfection can lead to anxiety, fostering an environment where individuals become hyper-aware of their perceived flaws in comparison to others. This can manifest in a detrimental cycle, where each swipe or message fuels insecurity and self-doubt. The fear of rejection becomes magnified, leading to avoidance behaviors rather than fostering resilience. This pattern not only alienates potential matches but also stifles personal growth and exploration. The quest for an ideal connection is overshadowed by a paralyzing fear of the imperfect, which ironically makes the prospect of dating more daunting than it needs to be. The desire for connection is compromised by excessive worry, limiting individuals from experiencing the joys and complexities of genuine interactions. The pitfalls of overthinking can distort the lens through which users view potential partners. With an abundance of choices available online, individuals might feel compelled to analyze compatibility through a hypercritical framework rather than embracing the organic development of relationships. As profiles are often curated to showcase the best aspects of an individual, reliance on superficial judgments becomes inevitable. Users may dismiss candidates based on minor discrepancies or selectiveness rather than recognizing the inherent value in each unique person they encounter. This narrow focus not only limits the possibilities for connections but may also contribute to a skewed perception of love and attachment, where the essence of partnership gets lost amid a sea of possibilities. Recognizing the hazards of overthinking is essential for fostering healthier relationships in the digital age, allowing individuals to approach dating with a sense of openness rather than apprehension.

## Misjudging Compatibility

In the fast-paced realm of online dating, users frequently fall prey to the allure of compatibility indicators that claim to foretell successful relationships. The systems in place rely heavily on self-reported data and standardized questionnaires designed to assess interests, values, and lifestyles. These algorithms churn through countless profiles, serving up matches that, on paper, may seem ideal; however, this numerical evaluation often oversimplifies the complex nature of human relationships. Emotional intelligence, chemistry, and the nuances of interpersonal interactions cannot merely be quantified through a series of questions or preferences. As a result, individuals may find themselves matched with partners who appear compatible yet lack the essential emotional connection or shared experiences that usually underpin successful relationships. Consequently, such miscalculations may lead users to dismiss compatible relationships that could have flourished in favor of those deemed more statistically aligned but ultimately disappointing. The tendency to misjudge compatibility is exacerbated by the superficiality embedded in online interactions. When individuals engage with potential partners primarily through curated profiles, they are often exposed to an edited version of reality. Not only do pictures and bios present a narrowed snapshot of someone's life, but they also allow users to project their desires onto those representations, leading to over-inflated expectations. This phenomenon is particularly pronounced in a digital landscape where first impressions are built upon photographs and selective information. When emotional and psychological dimensions of compatibility are overlooked in favor of eye-catching aesthetics or shared interests, the likelihood of discovering a meaningful connection diminishes. Users may pursue relationships more vigorously with those who fit an idealized vision rather than those who can genuinely engage with their emotional needs and long-term aspirations, resulting in a cycle of unfulfilling matches. Understanding the implications of misjudging compatibility is essential for users hoping to navigate the digital dating landscape with greater awareness. It is crucial to foster a mindset that prioritizes personal connection and emotional resonance over algorithm-driven forecasts. Approaching dating with curiosity and openness can unveil deeper compatibility that algorithms may overlook. Engaging in meaningful conversations and spending time together in real life can reveal shared values and interests that might not be immediately apparent through profiles alone. By managing expectations and recognizing that relationships require nurturing beyond the initial match, individuals can learn to appreciate the unique complexities that define genuine compatibility. Thus, as individuals become more discerning about what truly constitutes a match, they enhance not only their dating experiences but also their chances of finding fulfilling and lasting relationships.

## Ignoring Red Flags

Within the realm of online dating, the phenomenon of overlooking warning signs has emerged as a significant issue. Many individuals entering the digital dating scene often find themselves entranced by the excitement of new connections, only to disregard behaviors that might signal potential red flags. These indicators, such as inconsistent communication, overly intense displays of affection early on, or evasive responses to personal inquiries, can serve as crucial clues regarding a persons true character. The romantic allure, intensified by a range of curated profiles and glossy photographs, can cloud judgment, leading one to rationalize concerning behaviors as mere quirks or mis-understandings. This dismissal often stems from a deep-seated desire for intimacy and validation, which online platforms prom-ise to deliver with unprecedented convenience. Recognizing such red flags is essential, as it can help individuals navigate the complexities of modern relationships with greater awareness and safety. As people continue to engage in electronic courtship, it becomes increasingly apparent that romantic relationships in-itiated online often lack the foundational elements of in-person interactions. The absence of non-verbal cues, critical in human communication, can exacerbate misunderstandings and amplify the difficulty of discerning authentic intentions. Consequently, individuals might ignore not only red flags but also genuine signs of compatibility. Inconsistent messaging patterns could be per-ceived merely as busy schedules or temporary distractions, ra-ther than as potential indicators of emotional unavailability. The immediacy and superficiality that characterizes many online da-ting platforms contribute to this tendency to overlook important signals, as users often prioritize initial impressions over deeper assessments. The challenge then becomes twofold: recognizing the myriad of nuances that accompany digital interactions while simultaneously holding onto the hope that one's ideal match may be just a screen tap away. Long-term consequences of ig-noring red flags can severely impact mental and emotional well-being, effectively distorting one's perception of love and relationships. Those who overlook these critical warning signs may find themselves ensnared in toxic dynamics, characterized by manipulation or emotional harm. This detrimental cycle can perpetuate feelings of inadequacy, leading individuals to question their self-worth and further complicating their pursuit of meaningful connections. The digital age, with its promises of abundant choices and potential partners, can ironically isolate individuals caught in these unhealthy patterns, fostering a disconnect from authentic connections. To counteract these effects, individuals must cultivate a balanced approach to online dating that includes vigilance concerning red flags, a commitment to self-awareness, and the establishment of boundaries. In fostering such an attitude, users can engage with the digital dating world from a position of empowerment, ultimately enhancing their journey toward fulfilling and genuine love experiences.

# XXVI. CONCLUSION

In examining the dynamics of online dating, it is clear that while digital platforms offer new avenues for connection, they also introduce complexities that can complicate genuine relationships. Users often find themselves navigating a landscape inundated with profiles that sometimes present curated versions of individuals rather than authentic representations. This discrepancy between expectation and reality can lead to disillusionment, particularly when individuals invest emotional energy based on what they perceive through a screen, which may be constructed rather than sincere. It becomes crucial to understand that the algorithms designed to help users find compatibility may inadvertently promote superficial judgments, prioritizing aesthetics over emotional or intellectual connections. As a consequence, potential relationships may falter before they even begin, emphasizing the need for a more thoughtful approach to online dating that values authenticity over mere appearance. The rapid pace of online interactions contributes to an environment where meaningful connections often struggle to flourish. The immediacy that dating apps promote can foster a sense of disposable romance, where users swipe through potential partners as if they are commodities rather than individuals with rich histories and unique attributes. This transactional view of dating can lead to a culture rooted in instant gratification, overshadowing the importance of patience and genuine interest in fostering relationships. Studies indicate that such environments frequently result in shallow interactions, with many users experiencing increased feelings of loneliness despite being constantly connected. As participants lose sight of the deeper qualities that foster lasting relationships, they may inadvertently perpetuate myths about love and companionship that are fueled by the instant nature of digital interactions. The culmination of this exploration into the realities of online dating reveals the urgent need for a shift in how individuals approach these platforms. It is essential for users to cultivate a mindset that prioritizes quality interactions over quantity, offering the potential for deeper connections and reduced disappointment. Engaging with online dating requires a critical awareness of both personal intentions and the inherent limitations of the medium, encouraging users to step beyond the illusion of the perfect match. By adopting a balanced perspective that recognizes both the benefits and drawbacks of online dating, individuals can navigate this modern courtship landscape more effectively, creating opportunities for real love and meaningful relationships rather than succumbing to societys often misleading narratives. Embracing this conscious approach can help demystify the common misconceptions about digital romance and ultimately lead to a more fulfilling dating experience.

## Summary of Key Findings

The investigation into online dating has unveiled a multifaceted landscape that complicates the notion of finding love effortlessly with today's technology. One significant finding is the prevalence of online dating platforms among diverse demographics, revealing a broad acceptance of these services in contemporary society. Research indicates that nearly 30% of adults have used an online dating service, with younger users showing the highest engagement levels. This widespread participation contradicts the stereotype of online dating as a last resort and suggests a new cultural norm where digital interaction precedes traditional courtship. While these platforms promise connections, the reality often includes inconsistent user experiences. Many users report frustration due to ghosting or mismatched expectations. This two-sided nature of online dating complicates the narrative of modern romance and invites users to reevaluate their motivations and desired outcomes in this digital arena. A pivotal analysis of user behavior on dating apps highlights the impact of algorithms on romantic encounters. The data reveal that these algorithms are not merely tools for connection; they actively shape the dating experience by prioritizing certain traits and preferences, often leading to superficial selections. Users tend to make swift judgments based on limited information, such as profile pictures and short bios, reinforcing a culture of immediacy. Consequently, a paradox emerges: while technology facilitates access to a broader pool of potential partners, it simultaneously engenders a superficial approach to relationships. This can skew individuals' perceptions of compatibility and ideal partnership. The reliance on curated profiles raises the question of authenticity, as users may construct idealized versions of themselves. Such dynamics potentially distort genuine romantic connections, creating a landscape where emotional fulfillment is less guaranteed than it might seem at first glance. The synthesis of these findings suggests that while digital dating offers unprecedented opportunities for connection, it also requires a critical and conscious approach. Users must navigate the tension between the allure of quick matches and the importance of substantial engagement. To mitigate the effects of superficial judgments and erroneous expectations, individuals are encouraged to prioritize transparency and intentionality in

189

their online interactions. This includes investing time in detailed conversations before meeting in person, as well as recognizing the limitations of profiles as reflections of true identity. By fostering a more authentic digital dating experience, users can not only enjoy the benefits of these platforms but also build meaningful relationships that stand the test of time. Understanding the complexities at play empowers users to approach online dating not just as a convenient option, but as a thoughtful journey toward finding love that resonates with their true selves.

## Reflection on Myths vs. Truths

The digital landscape plays a pivotal role in shaping modern romantic relationships, often leading to the perpetuation of certain myths that cloud users perceptions. One prevalent belief is that online dating guarantees an instant connection and the possibility of meeting one's soul mate. This notion is heavily promoted by dating platforms that emphasize compatibility algorithms and success stories, giving users the impression that love is merely a few clicks away. Research indicates that while these platforms can provide opportunities to meet people, the reality is more complex. An overwhelming number of profiles can lead to decision fatigue, diminishing the quality of connections made. Instead of fostering meaningful relationships, users may find themselves in a cycle of superficial interactions, where genuine compatibility is overlooked in favor of aesthetics and fleeting first impressions. This disconnect between expectation and reality is crucial to understand for anyone navigating the world of online dating. There exists a myth that the anonymity afforded by online platforms fosters a safe environment for genuine interactions. In truth, this detachment can lead to deception, as individuals may curate an idealized version of themselves that doesn't reflect reality. Studies have shown that a significant portion of profiles contains misleading information, whether through edited photos or embellished descriptions, which can undermine trust right from the outset. This discrepancy can fuel disappointment and anxiety when the reality of a date does not align with its online representation. The pressure to present a polished self can lead to feelings of inadequacy among users, creating a culture of comparison that further complicates their quest for genuine connection. It becomes evident that the very mechanisms designed to facilitate relationships can also generate barriers that inhibit authenticity, emphasizing the need for skepticism regarding online personas. Distinguishing between myths and truths in online dating requires a nuanced perspective that embraces both the advantages and pitfalls of these platforms. While online dating can indeed expand one's social network and offer diverse opportunities for connection, it is crucial for users to ground their expectations in reality. Educating oneself about the inherent complexities of digital interactions can empower individuals to approach these platforms with an open mind and a critical eye. Strategies such as verifying profiles, seeking honest communication, and being patient in the process can significantly enhance the likelihood of finding meaningful relationships. By dispelling the myths and acknowledging the truths of online dating, users can navigate the digital romance landscape more effectively, ultimately fostering connections that are both fulfilling and authentic. These reflections on myths versus truths serve not only as guidance for individuals seeking love online but also as a reminder of the importance of realism in the pursuit of genuine connection in a rapidly evolving digital world.

## Recommendations for Online Daters

Building a genuine connection in the world of online dating requires deliberate efforts beyond just swiping left or right. Users must approach profiles with a critical and discerning eye. It is crucial to look for compatibility markers that extend beyond surface-level traits, such as shared interests and values. Exploring deeper aspects, like life goals and emotional availability, can significantly enhance the likelihood of forming a meaningful relationship. While profiles often highlight appealing images and catchy bios, individuals should not rely solely on these representations. Engaging in conversations that probe personal beliefs and experiences can establish a more accurate understanding of potential partners, laying the foundation for a deeper connection that transcends initial attraction. Safety is paramount in the online dating landscape, and taking precautions should be a priority for anyone participating in these platforms. One of the foremost recommendations is to keep personal information private until a solid level of trust is established. That can include refraining from sharing details such as home addresses, phone numbers, or financial information early in the communication. Users should consider meeting in public spaces for initial dates to ensure safety and comfort. Trusting one's instincts and being alert to red flags, such as evasive answers or inconsistencies in stories, can further protect users from deceitful encounters. Addressing these safety concerns is vital, allowing individuals to enjoy the excitement of meeting new people without compromising their well-being. Managing expectations is another essential component for success in online dating. Users often approach dating apps with the hope of quickly finding "the one," but this mindset can lead to disappointment. Recognizing that building a lasting relationship often takes time is crucial. Individuals should cultivate patience and an open mind, embracing the journey of dating rather than fixating exclusively on end results. Instead of focusing entirely on matchmaking algorithms that may promise instant connections, it might be more fruitful to view each interaction as an opportunity for learning and personal growth. By setting realistic expectations, online daters can enhance their experiences, open themselves up to various outcomes, and take pride in the connections they create, regardless of how long-lasting they may ultimately be.

## Final Thoughts on the Future of Online Dating

As society continues to evolve, the landscape of romantic relationships is shifting in ways that were previously unimaginable. Online dating has emerged as a predominant mode for meeting potential partners, driven by accessibility and the proliferation of mobile technology. This transformation, however, goes beyond mere convenience; it reflects changing networking norms and expectations about intimacy in an increasingly digital world. Emerging studies indicate that users often approach online platforms with heightened hopes of finding an ideal match, yet many grapple with the challenge of navigating a space rife with unrealistic portrayals and the potential for superficial connections. As individuals engage with dating apps, the blend of anonymity and curated profiles can lead to inflated expectations that seldom align with the complexities of genuine relationships. Consequently, future interactions will require a degree of clarity and self-awareness to maximize the benefits of these platforms while mitigating inherent risks. The future of online dating hinges on how both users and developers respond to evolving social dynamics and technological advancements. As algorithms continue to refine their matchmaking processes, there's an increasing emphasis on personalized experiences that cater to a wider range of preferences, lifestyles, and emotional needs. This burgeoning reliance on technology raises critical questions concerning authenticity and depth in connections. Potential issues, such as the commodification of love and the persistence of performative behavior, risk eroding the very essence of human interactions. New features designed to cultivate deeper emotional connections may inadvertently reinforce objectification or surface-level engagement, creating a paradox that complicates the path to genuine intimacy. As we venture into this uncharted territory, stakeholders in the online dating ecosystem must remain vigilant and proactive in fostering relationships founded on authenticity rather than algorithms alone. Constructing meaningful connections in the digital age requires a departure from idealized notions of romance typically perpetuated by online platforms. Education and awareness surrounding the myths of online dating can empower users to adopt a balanced perspective when engaging with these technologies. Its essential for individuals to cultivate realistic expectations and acknowledge that the pursuit of love online is just one way to connect, albeit a complex and nuanced one. A critical aspect of future trends will involve prioritizing honesty in self-presentation and communication to foster deeper relationships that withstand the test of time. Embracing vulnerability and authenticity may become the cornerstones for developing healthier relationships in a digital world that can often feel impersonal. As we move forward, the dialogue around online dating must evolve to emphasize the value of human connection over convenient algorithms, promoting a dating culture that honors the intricacies of love in all its forms.

# REFERENCES

Dan Slater. 'Love in the Time of Algorithms.' What Technology Does to Meeting and Mating, Penguin, 1/24/2013

Katharine Smyth. 'All the Lives We Ever Lived.' Seeking Solace in Virginia Woolf, Crown, 1/21/2020

Prof Tom C Clark. 'The Art of Lasting Love.' A Guide to Healthy Relationships, Amazon Digital Services LLC - Kdp, 12/23/2022

Lauren Rosewarne. 'Intimacy on the Internet.' Media Representations of Online Connections, Routledge, 4/14/2016

Charles John. 'Readiness for Marriage.' How to Determine Whether You Are Ready for Marriage, Amazon Digital Services LLC - Kdp, 2/7/2024

Michael Todd. 'Relationship Goals.' How to Win at Dating, Marriage, and Sex, Random House Publishing Group, 4/28/2020

Daniel Goleman. 'Self-Awareness (HBR Emotional Intelligence Series).' Harvard Business Review, Harvard Business Press, 11/13/2018

Caleb Gardner. 'No Point B.' Rules for Leading Change in the New Hyper-Connected, Radically Conscious Economy, BenBella Books, 8/9/2022

Patricia Page. 'Friends Or Lovers?.' 32 Signs that Indicate Your Best Friend Wants to Get in Bed with You, Amazon Digital Services LLC - Kdp, 6/27/2022

Jason S. Wrench. 'The Impact of Social Media in Modern Romantic Relationships.' Narissra M. Punyanunt-Carter, Lexington Books, 4/26/2017

Richard Wentk. 'iOS App Development Portable Genius.' John Wiley & Sons, 6/22/2012

Shah, Vrushank. 'Handbook of Research on AI-Based Technologies and Applications in the Era of the Metaverse.' Khang, Alex, IGI Global, 7/3/2023

Marie Bergström. 'The New Laws of Love.' Online Dating and the Privatization of Intimacy, John Wiley & Sons, 12/21/2021

Logan Ury. 'How to Not Die Alone.' The Surprising Science That Will Help You Find Love, Simon and Schuster, 2/2/2021

Wilasinee Pananakhonsab. 'Love and Intimacy in Online Cross-Cultural Relationships.' The Power of Imagination, Springer, 11/16/2016

Daniel S George. 'Love Beyond Borders.' Cultural Differences in Relationships, Amazon Digital Services LLC - Kdp, 5/1/2023

Dana Lützow. 'Online Dating – A cross-cultural comparison of matchmaking websites in the United States of America, Germany, India, and Japan.' GRIN Verlag, 1/4/2013

Susan C. South. 'Interpersonal Relationships and Health.' Social and Clinical Psychological Mechanisms, Christopher Rolfe Agnew, Oxford University Press, 1/1/2014

S C Wise. 'Relationship Goals.' Become Your Relationship Goal, Independently Published, 6/29/2020

Élisabeth Pacherie. 'Conscious Intentions.' The Social Creation Myth, Johannes Gutenberg-Universität Mainz, 1/1/2016

Steven Buck. 'Owl stretching and other issues... a self help manual.' Navigating Teenage Life: Your Comprehensive Guide to Overcoming Challenges and Thriving, Grosvenor House Publishing, 3/21/2024

Keengwe, Jared. 'Handbook of Research on Active Learning and Student Engagement in Higher Education.' IGI Global, 6/10/2022

Miguel Carvalho Abrantes. 'Against Online Dating.' Why can't you find true love?, Miguel Carvalho Abrantes, 12/25/2018

W. Ickes. 'Compatible and Incompatible Relationships.' Springer Science & Business Media, 12/6/2012

Kristan Higgins. 'The Perfect Match.' HQN Books, 10/29/2013

Corey Wayne. 'How to Be a 3% Man, Winning the Heart of the Woman of Your Dreams.' Lulu.com, 1/22/2006

Jacob C. Warren, PhD, MBA, CRA. 'Rural Mental Health.' Issues, Policies, and Best Practices, K. Bryant Smalley, PhD, PsyD, MBA, Springer Publishing Company, 6/20/2012

Meredith A. Newman. 'Emotional Labor.' Putting the Service in Public Service, Mary E. Guy, Routledge, 12/18/2014

John J. Evoy. 'The Rejected.' Psychological Consequences of Parental Rejection, Pennsylvania State University Press, 1/1/1981

Jonice Webb. 'Running on Empty No More.' Transform Your Relationships with Your Partner, Your Parents & Your Children, Morgan James Publishing, 11/7/2017

Sharron Hinchliff. 'Addressing the Sexual Rights of Older People.' Theory, Policy and Practice, Catherine Barrett, Routledge, 11/2/2017

Ashton Applewhite. 'This Chair Rocks.' A Manifesto Against Ageism, Celadon Books, 3/5/2019

NARAYAN CHANGDER. 'DIGITAL COMMUNICATION.' THE AMAZING QUIZ BOOK, Changder Outline, 2/28/2024

Carrie Henderson McDermott. 'He Texted.' The Ultimate Guide to Decoding Guys, Lisa Winning, Simon and Schuster, 10/7/2014

Gustavo Cardoso. 'Online/offline : Can You Tell the Difference?.' Portuguese Views on Internet Mediated Communication, Vita e pensiero, 1/1/2002

Marie Sinclair Countess of Caithness. 'Old Truths in a New Light, Or, An Earnest Endeavour to Reconcile Material Science with Spiritual Science, and with Scripture.' By the Countess of Caithness, Chapman and Hall, 1/1/1876

John D. Surma. 'Occupational Safety and Health Law Handbook.' Bernan Press, 11/30/2023

Competition Bureau Canada. 'The Little Black Book of Scams.' Your Guide to Protection Against Fraud, The Canadian Edition, Industry Canada, Competition Bureau Canada, 3/10/2014

John C. Bridges. 'The Illusion of Intimacy.' Problems in the World of Online Dating, Bloomsbury Publishing USA, 5/15/2012

David F. Manlove. 'Algorithmics of Matching Under Preferences.' World Scientific, 1/1/2013

Ricardo Colomo-Palacios. 'Electronic Business and Marketing.' New Trends on its Process and Applications, Tokuro Matsuo, Springer, 4/6/2013

David Beer. 'The Social Power of Algorithms.' Routledge, 10/23/2019

Clint Stonebraker. 'Connected:The Art of Building Relationships.' Clint Stonebraker, 10/1/2009

Claire Hultin. 'Love, Sex & Deception.' The Chronicles of Online Dating, Morgan James Publishing, 7/15/2010

Wind Song. 'Miss Match.' Volume 1, Funstory, 12/16/2019

Dina C. Maramba. 'The Misrepresented Minority.' New Insights on Asian Americans and Pacific Islanders, and the Implications for Higher Education, Samuel D. Museus, Taylor & Francis, 7/3/2023

J. O. Robinson. 'The Psychology of Visual Illusion.' Courier Corporation, 1/18/2013

Michael Thomas Neubert. 'The Effects of Selection and Emphasis Upon Reader Responses to News Pictures.' University of Wisconsin--Madison, 1/1/1966

Jennifer Mather Saul. 'Lying, Misleading, and What is Said.' An Exploration in Philosophy of Language and in Ethics, OUP Oxford, 10/25/2012

Katherine Chandler Yonge. 'Criminal Profile Accuracy Following Training in Inductive and Deductive Approaches.' Mississippi State University, 1/1/2008

George R. Goethals. 'Theories of Group Behavior.' Brian Mullen, Springer Science & Business Media, 12/6/2012

Paul J. D'Ambrosio. 'You and Your Profile.' Identity After Authenticity, Hans-Georg Moeller, Columbia University Press, 5/25/2021

Navaratna Srinivasa Rajaram. 'Profiles in Deception.' Ayodhya and the Dead Sea Scrolls, Voice of India, 1/1/2000

United States. 'United States Code.' Office of the Law Revision Counsel of the House of Representatives, 1/1/2013

Kamal Ravikant. 'Live Your Truth.' Kamal Ravikant, 7/1/2013

Shimrit Elisar. 'Everyone's Guide To Online Dating.' How to Find Love and Friendship on the Internet, Little, Brown Book Group, 5/25/2007

Erika Ettin. 'Love at First Site.' Tips and Tales for Online Dating Success from a Modern-Day Matchmaker, Greenleaf Book Group, 9/2/2014

Sean Calvin Aaron. 'Investigating Motivations for Using Dating Websites and Geosocial Apps.' Brigham Young University. Department of Psychology, 1/1/2017

Leslie Parrott. 'dot.com dating.' finding your right someone online--avoiding the liars, losers, and freaks, Les Parrott, Tyndale House Publishers, Inc., 5/3/2011

Matt A Mayer. 'The Myth of the Bigger, Better Deal.' One Guy's View on Why Dating Apps Make Dating Harder, Amazon Digital Services LLC - Kdp, 2/27/2024

Syd Logan. 'Cross-Platform Development in C++.' Building Mac OS X, Linux, and Windows Applications, Pearson Education, 11/27/2007

Lizeth Elena Lomeli. 'Online Dating.' Kiss Or Miss? Exploring the Trends Amongst Millennial People of Color, Amber Castillo Cordero, California State University, Northridge, 1/1/2020

Amy Webb. 'Data, a Love Story.' How I Cracked the Online Dating Code to Meet My Match, Penguin, 1/28/2014

Liz Woods. 'Pros and Cons of Online Dating.' Independently Published, 3/28/2020

Eric Klinenberg. 'Modern Romance.' Aziz Ansari, Penguin, 6/14/2016

Michael Lasky. 'Online Dating For Dummies.' Judith Silverstein, John Wiley & Sons, 3/8/2011

Carl-Adam Wachtmeister. 'The Evolution of Courtship Rituals.' Department of Zoology [Zoologiska institutionen], Univ., 1/1/2000

Nichi Hodgson. 'The Curious History of Dating.' From Jane Austen to Tinder, Little, Brown Book Group, 1/26/2017

Gregory Allen Schrempp. 'The Truth of Myth.' World Mythologies in Theory and Everyday Life, Tok Thompson, Oxford University Press, 1/1/2020

Lynn Stafford-Yilmaz. 'Writers at Work: The Essay Student's Book.' The Essay, Dorothy Zemach, Cambridge University Press, 1/14/2008

Heather Vernita. 'Navigating Online Dating.' Expert Advice On Proven Techniques And Insights To Find Your Perfect Match While Loving In The Digital Age, Amazon Digital Services LLC - Kdp, 11/5/2023

Kelly J Mays. 'The Norton Introduction to Literature.' Twelfth Edition, W. W. Norton & Company, 10/8/2015

www.ingramcontent.com/pod-product-compliance
Lightning Source LLC
Chambersburg PA
CBHW052315220526
45472CB00001B/122